SEASHORE
ENTERTAINING

SEASHORE ENTERTAINING

NAOMI BLACK

A QUARTO BOOK

RUNNING PRESS
BOOK PUBLISHERS
PHILADELPHIA, PENNSYLVANIA

A RUNNING PRESS/QUARTO BOOK

Canadian representatives: General Publishing, 30 Lesmill Road, Don Mills, Ontario M3B 2T6. International representatives: Worldwide Media Services, Inc. 115 East Twenty-Third Street, New York, NY 10016

9 8 7 6 5 4 3 2 1

Digit on the right indicates the number of this printing.

Library of Congress Cataloging-in-Publication Data
Black, Naomi, 1957-
Seashore entertaining.
Includes index.
1. Entertaining.   2. Cookery.   3. Seashore.
I. Title.
TX731.B56   1987   642'.4   86-28051
ISBN 0-89471-506-2 Cloth

SEASHORE ENTERTAINING
was prepared and produced by
Quarto Marketing Ltd.
15 West 26th Street
New York, New York 10010

Editor: Louise Quayle
Art Director: Mary Moriarty
Photo Editor: Susan M. Duane
Production Manager: Karen L. Greenberg
Mechanicals: Lisa Kenny and Debra Drovillo

Typeset by I CLAVDIA, Inc.
Color separations by Hong Kong Scanner Craft Company Ltd.
Printed and bound in Hong Kong by Leefung-Asco Printers Ltd.

This book may be ordered from the publisher. Please include $1.50 postage.
But try your bookstore first.

Running Press Book Publishers
125 South Twenty-Second Street
Philadelphia, Pennsylvania 19103

For Susannah,
whose love for cooking is just beginning.

ACKNOWLEDGMENTS

Acknowledgments are due to the following restaurants and publishers for their generous permission to use their recipes:

The Ark Restaurant of Nahcotta, Washington, and Ladysmith Limited Publishing Company, St. Louis, Missouri, who originally published *The Ark Restaurant Cookbook* in 1983.
Café 43 of New York City
Elizabeth on 37th of Savannah, Georgia
Joe's Stone Crab Restaurant of Miami Beach, Florida
The Manhattan Ocean Club of New York City
Maryland Office of Seafood Marketing, Department of Economic and Community Development
The Mooring of Newport, Rhode Island
South Carolina Division of Tourism
The Rogue of Monterey, California
The Sardine Factory of Monterey, California
Square One of San Francisco, California
Torremolinos Restaurant of New York City
West Beach Café of Venice, California

And to the chefs and owners: among them, Jimella Lucas, Nanci Main, Michael and Elizabeth Terry, Steve Mellina, Philip Larson, Bill Hufferd, Bert Cutino, and Joyce Goldstein.

Thanks must also go to Ray Hagan, who through the National Tabletop Association helped us to gather props for our photo shoots. And to the companies whose products we borrowed: MacKenzie-Childs; Le Jacquard Française; Ed Gillies for Contempo; Haeger Decorative Accessories; Prado Glassware; Royal Crystal Rock; Charles Sadek Import Co. Inc.; Un Jardin En Plus; Josiah Wedgwood and Sons, Inc.; Waechtersbach; The Wilton Company; and WMF of America, Inc. A special thanks to stylist James Goslee III, photographer Jeff MacNamara, and Don Kramer. Thanks also to Judd Pilossof, Gordon Smith, Sandra DosPassos, Paul Wheeler, and the Cisco Sisters.

A very special thanks goes to B.B. Bralower, wine consultant, who selected the wines and champagnes in Chapter One. Thanks are also due to Jamie Harrison who contributed a number of the recipes.

And grateful acknowledgment must go also to Mary Moriarty, Karla Olson, and last but not least, my most talented editor, Louise Quayle. Thanks, too, to Lizzie Grossman, Judy Habegger, and Rachel Christmas. And to John Bralower.

AUTHOR'S NOTE

This book is as much an idea book as it is a practical guide on how to cook fish and shellfish. The photographs throughout act as a counterpoint to the text, illustrating additional ways to present delicacies from the sea. The recipes in the cooking chapter, many of which are adapted classics, are arranged so you can try the cooking techniques. If your imagination is sparked and you are no longer afraid to experiment with fish and shellfish, then this book will have served its purpose.

CONTENTS

CHAPTER ONE

GREAT MEALS IN GREAT ENVIRONMENTS

ENTERTAINING NOTES

Miss Manners, author of *Miss Manners' Guide to Excruciatingly Correct Behavior,* has rejected the common secret of success for a perfect party—good food and interesting people—and redefined it: "It should be full of tension." She's right, but the stimulating tension created by guests getting to know one another is quite different from the stress some hosts and hostesses display when they don't plan well for a party. If fate is in your favor, advance planning is the key to a flawless party. But an impromptu get-together has not lost its place in the world of entertaining either. Just set aside some time for gathering your thoughts about how best to approach a meal, even if the final decision leads you to the nearest deli for smoked fish and cold cuts. When you're entertaining you have to make the most of what you have, whether that's time, ingredients, or skill.

The meals included in this chapter range from the very simple to the ornate. Some menus necessitate long hours spent in the kitchen; others, only an hour or so for shopping and less than that for final preparation.

The table settings also vary from informal to *haute,* offering ideas that you can incorporate into your own schemes. The pages within this chapter are feats for the eyes: the dishes and setups reflect the very best work of stylists and photographers. Your own home can be transformed just as easily if you give thought to lighting, color, shape (of tables, chairs, dishes, even foods), and atmosphere. This last element is often forgotten, but in some ways it is the most important factor in putting together a memorable meal. Your dining room breakfront may be stocked with the finest china, but it still may not hold exactly what you want for a certain meal: it doesn't matter. Inject the elegance, humor, whimsy, or whatever with small props set around the table—in the centerpiece, as placecards, by the napkins. Let your imagination be sparked by the ideas here and go from there.

Table Settings

The term *china* is used loosely here to include everything from fine porcelain to hearty earthenware to glass and plastics. When you plan your table settings you'll want at least one full set of china that you can use as a formal base. Having a service plate, or underplate, a necessity with formal dinners, is a nice touch even for an informal meal. (Conventionally, the service plate should be removed when the heated dinner plate is placed on the table.) Mix and match according to your taste, but consider how the food will look with each plate. Serving dishes may match the china, but this is not necessary.

If you are a true seafood addict, you may want to consider investing in plates with a scallop shell or nautical motif. Tableware designed for fish cookery is gaining prominence. Besides individual shrimp cocktail services, there are scallop shells —natural and porcelain; fish appetizer plates that are long and narrow; personal-size soufflé dishes and fish-shaped molds; even one-serving Chinese steam baskets that are perfect for a dinner of pan-dressed fish, vegetables, and Oriental noodles.

Flatware varies from formal sets that include salad forks and butter knives to informal arrangements that include Chinese porcelain soup spoons or plastic forks. Fish forks and knives supplement a formal table setting, but are unnecessary for most meals; just make sure that there is a clean utensil for each course of the meal. If you plan to serve lobster, crackers and picks round out the setting, as a cocktail fork does for shrimp cocktail.

Relax

Both anticipated feasts with picnic utensils and unexpected dinners with fine china share one crucial rule: relax. That fact hasn't changed. In the 1928 version of *For the Hostess: A Handbook for Entertaining,* the author states, "Of course, it is a somewhat more simple matter to advise ease of manner and perfect tranquillity in the face of any unforeseen occurrences from the printed page of a book than it is to practice them on every occasion. But it is true that the woman who cultivates or has been endowed...with these qualities, together with a natural friendliness and courtesy towards her guests, is the one who makes the nearest approach to being the perfect hostess." Putting your feet up for just half an hour and, more important, clearing your head of all the details of the party, can be the one factor that makes you calm and the event successful.

Books, magazines, family, and friends do tend to go on and on about relaxing and taking mishaps in stride. It *is* easier said than done, but the advice should be heeded by everyone who wants to entertain with grace and style. These tips may help.

- Be meticulous but flexible when making and following plans. Don't make lists and forget them. On the other hand, don't allow yourself to panic if the store doesn't have what you need; calmly come up with alternatives and choose one solution even if it doesn't match a preconceived notion in your mind.

- Keep the party as simple as you can with only one complex or elaborate touch.

- Determine a budget and stay within your limits.

- Invite at least one friend who you can rely on to help out if "disaster" strikes. A quick hug in the kitchen from a good friend or relative can be as helpful as the services of a hired caterer or cleanup person.

- With such good quality foods on the market today, don't be ashamed to supplement your home cooking with a store-bought or mail-order delicacy. Make sure, however, that you know the company is reliable and that the food is excellent.

- *Don't overextend yourself!* Attempt to do only what you can do.

With few exceptions, you'll be entertaining for friends, so if something unfortunate happens, smile, be gracious, and laugh. If you handle the situation well, so will the guests and the party will continue smoothly.

If you're outside and serving steamed lobster or steamed crab claws, brightly colored paper goods and plastic utensils can be a practical alternative to china. Choose high-quality, coated plates that won't bend when exposed to moisture.

Jeff McNamara (James Goslee III, stylist)

DOWNEAST CLAMBAKE

Robert Mondavi White Blush Zinfandel 1985 (California)

The coast of Maine enchants. Rockbound shores nudge up against seaside towns. Windjammers ply the waters around Camden, lighthouses at Pemaquid Point and Owls Head attract artists in droves, and seafood abounds in the fingers of ocean and river that form the seaboard. The rough beauty of Maine lures artists and artisans as well as those seeking solitude.

Maine is one of the few places where you can still forage for the basics of a clambake. Starting out early in the morning after checking the tides, you can gather clams, set out lobster pots, and pluck a few mussels off their perch as you look for rockweed and stones. A stop at the nearest vegetable stand would fill out the menu, but you could make do with just seafare.

More likely, you'll plan a visit to your local fish market and place an order for at least a 1-pound lobster per person and a dozen steamers each. At the grocery, get two ears of corn, a potato or two, and an onion per person. Throw in a pound of sausage for every four people, and you'll have reason to provide blankets and pillows for everyone after the meal. The only other necessities are a shovel for digging the pit; metal buckets to hold water and spent coals; hardwood and/or driftwood; matches; 20 to 30 pounds of rockweed (collect or order at the fish market); and a tarp for covering the pit.

Before you get to the beach, if you can manage it, scrub and soak the clams in sea water with a bit of cornmeal for a few hours (see page 106), strip the corn down to the tender green husks, and wash the potatoes and check for bad spots.

To begin, dig a pit in the sand above the tideline, the dimensions of which should run approximately 2½ feet by 4 feet by 2½ or 3 feet deep. Collect stones from the area to line the pit—flat-sided specimens about 5 inches thick are best. (Do not use shale or sedimentary rock; they may explode when heated.) Then pile the wood in the pit, make a bonfire, and let it burn for 2 or 3 hours; when most if not all of the wood has burned and the coals

Incorporate traditional wood lobster traps into the design scheme: fill one with flowers to create a decorative side piece.

become ash-white, scoop out the unburned wood and the ash, leaving the hot stones.

Now you have to act quickly. Place a layer of rockweed, the type of seaweed that holds moisture best, on the stones. (If you want you can put down a length of dampened cheesecloth on top of each layer of seaweed, but it's not traditional.) First lay the clams and sausage down, cover with more rockweed, add the sweet potatoes, then another lighter layer of rockweed. Next in are the new potatoes, onions, and sweet corn, followed by one last layer of rockweed and the lobsters. Cover all with a tarp that has been soaking in the sea water, and secure it with rocks.

Whether you opt for cabanas, umbrellas, tents, or the open air, keep the table simple. A picnic table is perfect, but you can improvise with a folding aluminum table. Cover the table with a country cloth—a checked pattern lends a homespun air. Carved out spots in the sand are the best chairs when you don't have a picnic bench. Use baskets to hold cutlery (plastic or stainless); cloth napkins that match the tablecloth and that do double-duty as lap cloths; and paper napkins for the real mess, which is inevitible. Sturdy paper plates are not an uncommon sight, nor are plastic glasses for beer and homemade lemonade.

If you want to make the occasion a little more elegant, bring all the food to the table. Otherwise, just serve from the pit itself. (One caution to the pit crew. The cooking area can be dangerous if not respected. Wear shoes, long pants, long sleeves, and gloves when at the pit.)

A clambake lends itself to elegance readily. With just the addition of stuffed potatoes and a spectacular dessert, the mood changes to one of refined dining.

Simple checked placemats—with solid blue cloth napkins—are casual, totable, and perfect for picnic settings.

An Indoor Clambake

The most important culinary effect of a clambake is the intermingling of flavors. Whether you're preparing a feast indoors or out, you want to produce a fragrant, almost heady steam in which to cook.

For an indoor clambake, you will need a large lobster steamer with an interior perforated basket (see Stockpots, page 72), aluminum foil, and the ingredients: steamers, sweet onions, small new potatoes, sweet corn, and lobsters. Wrap the onions, potatoes, and shucked corn in individual packets of foil. Fill the pot with enough water so that 1 inch of the basket is submerged; bring to a boil. If you can get your hands on some seaweed, clean it and line the bottom of the basket with it. If not, just add the wrapped potatoes. Cover and steam for 15 minutes; add more hot water or 1/2 cup sherry at this point.

Place a layer of wet cheesecloth on top of the potatoes and put the lobsters on top of the potatoes and put the lobsters on top of this. Cover and steam for 10 minutes; add the corn (and more water, if necessary), cover, and steam for an additional 8 minutes.

For the final step, lay down more wet cheesecloth as a carpet for the cleaned steamers; add the clams, cover, and steam until the clams open, between 5 and 10 minutes.

The cheesecloth will make disassembling the clambake easier. Use tongs or padded kitchen mitts to remove the items. Serve with side dishes of melted butter and lemon wedges.

NIGHT'S END IN NEWPORT

Late-Night Snack for a Crowd

Twisted Cheese Breadsticks
Clam Chowder
Poached Brandied Pears
Almond Crescent Cookies

Remy Martin

If you're more ambitious, try making a chunky fish and mussel stew seasoned with dill, instead of a clam chowder.

Before Newport became known as a private resort for the very rich it was "a quiet farming and fishing community where a few Southern planters, New England intellectuals, and staid New Yorkers vacationed casually in modest dwellings. For amusement summer visitors sailed, rode horses, fished, walked along the cliff above the ocean, or swam, with everyone in colorful bathing dresses looking—according to…Julia Ward Howe —like 'a ragged rainbow.'"

The city has changed and transformed from the community described by David Black in *The King of Fifth Avenue* to the sparkling colony that fostered the building of the grand mansions: the lavish, Chateau-sur-Mer, one of America's finest examples of Victorian architecture; the Breakers, a 72-room beauty styled after a northern Italian palazzo for Cornelius Vanderbilt; the Stanford White designed terra-cotta manse, Rosecliff, modeled to look like the Grand Trianon at Versailles; and more. The houses are now under the jurisdiction of the Preservation Society of Newport County and are open to the public during the summer and on weekends in the winter. The days of grandeur have become tame.

The summer sun still encourages long hours spent strolling, playing, and sitting back. The cool summer air further stimulates activity. When the night closes in and you've finally decided to return home, take a tip from the parties of yore. Offer your guests a light midnight snack as they unwind.

Everything but the clam chowder can be prepared beforehand, and the pears practically take care of themselves. Poach them in sugared water until they're firm but easily pierced. Reduce the sugared water, add the brandy at the last minute, drizzle on the pears, and serve.

Set the table buffet style and offer individual tray tables or lap trays for each guest. Use lace and linen with the most delicate flowers of the season as a nod to the turn-of-the-century entertainers. Lay out your best silver serving trays and cutlery; accent with low statuary, a favorite antique, or a large shell filled with a spray of yellow freesia and lilac. Offer brandy to those who wish a nightcap. Then bid everyone goodnight and pleasant dreams of cool summer breezes.

As a non-alcoholic alternative, poached pears are just as nice when glazed with syrup (above). The regal Breakers, with its Italian façade and meticulously groomed lawn, overlooks the majestic cliffs of Newport, Rhode Island (right).

Clamming for Joy

Deck yourself out in your Sunday best: sneakers or rubber boots, a warm shirt if you start out in the morning, and the oldest pair of comfortable pants you have. Then hit the beach. Soft-shell clams like mud or sand-and-mud; look for their hideouts by the bubbles and squirts around your feet as you walk the tidal flats at low tide. Plant yourself in the middle of an area that has lots of activity and with a garden fork turn the sand over, working your way around in a circle. Or, you can feel around with your toes, but this method is just a tad unreliable. A clam rake is the most efficient, but it takes away some of the challenge, and you shouldn't rake amid vegetation.

Hunt for quahogs in much the same way, but dig down about 6 to 12 inches to find them.

THE MOORING'S CLAM CHOWDER

Chef Philip Larson has won awards for his version of a New England classic. Right on the water, The Mooring restaurant epitomizes an air of casual elegance, an air that permeates Newport of the 1980s.

Roux:
1/2 cup salted butter
3 cups diced Spanish onions
1 cup all-purpose flour

Stock:
1 quart minced sea clams
1 1/2 quarts unsalted natural clam juice
1 1/2 quarts half & half
1 pound peeled diced potatoes
Spanish paprika for garnish

Melt the butter in a 1 1/2-gallon heavy stockpot. Add the onions and sauté until clear. Blend in flour and cook over low heat, stirring frequently for 2 to 4 minutes. Set aside to cool.

In a separate pot, bring to a boil clams and clam juice. Let simmer for 15 to 20 minutes. In another pot, cook the peeled diced potatoes just until soft in boiling water. Drain and set aside.

Add hot stock to the cooled roux and whisk thoroughly until smooth. Slowly bring to a boil. Reduce heat and add cooked potatoes. Carefully whisk (do not smash potatoes) in about 2/3 of the half & half, or more to taste. Simmer for 5 to 10 minutes. Ladle into warmed soup bowls. Sprinkle with a dash of Spanish paprika. **Serves approximately 20 as a first course; 10 to 15 as a midnight snack.**

MORNING IN MARYLAND

Breakfast for Four

Popovers and Croissants
Maryland Crab Meat Omelet
Summer Fruit Compote

Beringer Chenin Blanc 1985 (California)

Nearly four thousand miles of shoreline and approximately five hundred sheltered harbors comprise the coast of Chesapeake Bay, one of the most productive bodies of water in the world. Beyond the bay lies the Eastern Shore and then Assateague Island National Seashore. With all this natural bounty there are still areas little known to many visitors. Calvert Cliffs State Park is one such place; on the lower Chesapeake, it includes thirty miles of fossil-rich cliffs that overlook the ocean.

Plan a day by the cliffs looking for fallen prehistoric shark teeth or—if Maryland is miles away—use the park as an inspiration for your decor. Set the breakfast table with pastel colors of sky, sea, and shell. Two tablecloths—one of green and one of blue—placed at angles on top of each other are a cheery morning reminder of the sea and sky. Or use a blue-and-white checked cloth such as the one shown. Collect fossils, minerals, and geodes to create a base for a small, simple vase of beach roses or pink cosmos. If children are at the table, hide the names of the rocks and fossils under plates and napkins, and ask them to match the name cards to the geological samples (have them put the name cards with the fossils, not vice versa).

Prepare the compote in advance and place in the serving dishes. Bring the popover ingredients to room temperature. Clean the crab meat. Mix the popover batter and bake; while the popovers are in the oven, make the omelet, so the two will be ready at the same time. Have a variety of jams on hand.

The meal reflects the simplicity of a resplendent morning brimming with expectation. If you're near the seashore, center the afternoon's activity on crabbing to replace the crab meat you used in the omelet.

Breakfast is a perfect meal to set out your favorite mix and match or one-of-a-kind dishes. Whimsy reigns. Here, a 1930s teapot shares the table with handpainted berry bowls from MacKenzie-Childs and Fiestaware pastel plates.

Good-Natured Crabbing

It's easy and everyone can join in, even the littlest member of the family. Blue crabs like muddy bay areas and estuaries, while the Dungeness crabs of the West Coast prefer sandy bottoms. Whichever catch you're after, check the state regulations for season, minimum size permitted, and quantity allowed. The basics for crabbing are the same on both coasts, but it seems that each region has its preference.

Buy a dip net and cord or line to start and ask where the crabs are biting. Tie a chicken neck to the bottom of the line and lower into the water. When you feel a nibble, bring the line up very slowly until the crab is almost to the surface of the water. While you're doing this, slowly slide the net into place below the crab. With one quick motion bring the net up quickly to capture the critter.

If you want to use a surer method, purchase a collapsible trap. (Easterners prefer a trap; Westerners, a crab ring.) Tie bait securely to the trap and lower into the water with an attached rope. Leave the trap and return periodically to check the catch. Children can help raise and lower the rope and feel they are contributing to the process.

A dark plate offers contrast to the yellow of a Maryland crab meat omelet served in a wedge. Keep garnishes to a minimum: a sprig of fresh mint for the fruit, parsley for the omelet.

MARYLAND CRAB MEAT OMELET FILLING

The blue crab, known for its "cussedness" as well as its canniness and strength, lies at the heart of many Maryland meals. The recipe below, adapted from The Maryland Outdoor Recreation Guide, *is simple and scrumptious, the perfect centerpiece to an early morning breakfast or late afternoon brunch.*

1 pound Maryland or other backfin crab meat
4 tablespoons butter
1 cup heavy cream
1 teaspoon chopped tarragon (fresh, if possible)
1/8 teaspoon hot pepper sauce

Remove cartilage from the crab meat. Melt the butter in a medium-size saucepan; add the crab meat and sauté gently until thoroughly heated. Add the heavy cream, tarragon, and hot pepper sauce. Cook over low heat until the sauce has a creamy consistency, stirring occasionally. Remove from the heat and set aside while making the omelets. **Makes filling for 4 omelets.**

When mixed together, different shades and patterns of the same color can produce a lovely, composed table setting. The all-white floral arrangement heightens the subtle drama of the table.

Jeff McNamara

A Festive Buffet for Six

She-Crab Soup *or*
Vol-au-Vents with Oysters
Cold Chicken, Ham, and Tongue
Fresh Rolls
Green Salad with Tomatoes
Medley of Whole Fresh Fruit
Dacquoise

With the vol-au-vents: Chablis 1er Cru 1984 Louis Michel Chablis (France)
With the chicken: Georges Du boeuf Chilled Beaujolais Village 1985 (France)

When James Beard was a child in the American Northwest one of his favorite meals was a late supper prepared by his mother for their friends: "*vol-au-vents* with creamed Olympia oysters—surely the most heavenly dish ever created" (*Delights and Prejudices*). The baked shells held a sauce of white wine, oyster liquor, cream, eggs, a little roux, and a dash of Madeira; the oysters, put in just prior to service barely had time to settle into the sauce. The meal continued with "cold chicken, ham and tongue, perhaps, good rolls, a salad, and either fruit or some cheese and white wine." In tribute to the great food writer, this menu embraces the meal of his memories. The combination works equally well with fresh seafare from the East Coast; you can substitute the she-crab soup for the *vol-au-vents* for entertaining with a more regional flair while maintaining the spirit of the event.

South Carolina celebrates its seafood with a gusto that would impress any gourmand. In one year the state has sponsored a Lobster Race and Oyster Parade, a Lowcountry Shrimp Festival that includes a "blessing of the fleet," a Blue Crab Arts and Crafts Festival, and a Spring Pier King Mackerel Fishing Tournament, among others. Its sister state to the north has a sumptuous array of seafood and sea festivals as well.

In addition to oysters, shrimp, lobster, crab, and mackerel, the Carolinas boast of bass, bluefish, clams, herring, mullet, puppy drum, rockfish, scallops, and shad. And that's only the beginning of the list. Celebrations seem as common as seashore delicacies, so set your buffet with a festive theme: hang kites up behind the buffet table or arrange an unusually full or beautiful floral centerpiece (for a good overview of contemporary floral design, see Hal Cook's *Arranging*, published by William Morrow, 1985). Charleston is known for its magnificent gardens—Cypress, Magnolia, and Middleton—lush and fragrant with azaleas, magnolias, and Spanish moss. Choose your stems and blossoms with those traditional flowers in mind. If you have the space you may even want to create an indoor flowerbox.

Use a tablecloth and dishes that pick up a delicate pattern of blooms or buds. Complementary underplates and bolder matching glassware brighten the room while adding depth to the color scheme.

Formality is the watchword at this table. A full setting of service plate, soup bowl, water goblets, and green colored glasses make for an elegant southern meal.

CHARLESTON SHE-CRAB SOUP

This recipe from South Carolina celebrates the state's links with the ocean. Amid its fifty-five miles of beaches, anyone can crab, swim, and dine in outdoor splendor.

$1/4$ pound butter
1 tablespoon flour
1 quart milk
2 cups white crab meat and roe
Few drops of onion juice
$1/2$ teaspoon Worcestershire sauce
Mace to taste
Salt and pepper to taste
4 tablespoons dry sherry
Whipped cream

Melt the butter and blend in the flour. Add the milk and blend until thick and smooth. Stir in the crab meat, roe, onion juice, Worcestershire, mace, salt, and pepper. Cook slowly for 20 minutes over hot water. Pour $1/2$ tablespoon warmed sherry into individual soup bowls. Add the soup. Top each bowl with a spoonful of whipped cream. Serve piping hot. **Serves 4.**

GEORGIA ON MY MIND

Ham Pithivers
Shrimp and Grouper Elizabeth
Broccoli Purée
Peach Cobbler and Vanilla Ice Cream

Sonoma Cutrer Chardonnay-Pusseau 1984 (California)
or Château St. Jean Sauvignon Blanc 1985 (California)

Georgia, a land of varying climate and terrain, evokes images of romance and politics, *Gone With the Wind* and Jimmy Carter. Georgia's stretch of coastline, which runs from Savannah to Cumberland Island National Seashore, is often forgotten for Atlanta or other, more prominent inland cities. The shoreline looks out on the islands once called the Golden Isles of Guale: Jekyll, Sapelo, and Blackbeard to name a few. The territory is rife with seafood and traditions.

White wicker and straw hats seem the order of the day, along with magnolias and cool, tall drinks. Un Jardin...En Plus has captured the essence of a summer's day in its line of table linens and tableware. Lavender, green, pink, and white soften a hot sun and bring a lushness equal to the area from which the featured recipe comes. Shrimp and Grouper Elizabeth will look even more appetizing when it's served on geranium plates with magnolia blossoms placed nearby. Miniature straw hats tied with pastel ribbons make good place cards if you want to lend a formal air to the dinner.

Plan to spend the morning cooking as this meal, unlike some of the others in *Seashore Entertaining,* requires that a fair amount of the day be spent preparing for the dinner. (A well-defined seating plan might help avoid confusion in the dining room when you're trying to finish up in the kitchen.) The pithivers, purée, and cobbler, however, will be at their best if made as soon to mealtime as possible. The Shrimp and Grouper Elizabeth also necessitates last-minute attention. In another room or a separate area of the porch, set out a plate of cheeses and pâtés served with water crackers, if you like, to distract your guests from the goings-on in the kitchen.

As a perfect finish to the dinner, bring out the cobbler in a footed dessert dish placed on a plate covered with a lace doily. You can use the lace motif in the centerpiece, too, by draping some of the material over the edge of a low vase filled with the freshest blooms of the season—an elegant but informal meal that's steeped in the stories of the South.

An on-the-porch setting with green lettuce leaf soup bowls, which are offset by a brightly colored tablecloth, seem to blend in with the greenery of the outdoors. The tall candlesticks add a hint of formality.

Lizzie Himmel

SHRIMP AND GROUPER ELIZABETH

Ranked as "the best restaurant on the Georgia Coast" by Atlanta *magazine, Elizabeth on 37th offers this elegant recipe using the inspired combination of delicate, white-fleshed grouper and fresh, firm shrimp.*

1 pound shrimp
1 pound skinless grouper fillet
2 to 3 carrots
2 to 3 zucchini
1 Spanish onion
1 bunch leeks (use the white plus 1 inch of green)
$^1/_2$ package of Pepperidge Farm or other puff pastry
3 tablespoons butter, melted, plus 2 tablespoons for assembly
2 tablespoons flour
1 cup heavy cream
1 tablespoon dry vermouth
$^1/_4$ cup V-8 juice
Grated peel of 1 lemon
1 tablespoon fresh lemon juice

Peel and devein the shrimp. Cube the grouper to the size of the shrimp. Set aside. Preheat the oven to 425 degrees.

Wash and cut the carrots, zucchini, onion, and leeks into julienne strips the size of matchsticks. Do not use the center of the zucchini as it will become too mushy when cooked. You will need about 3 cups of mixed vegetables. Set aside.

Cut one sheet of the pastry into 4 squares. Bake on a greased cookie sheet for 10 minutes, until golden and puffed. Split and reserve.

Combine the 3 tablespoons melted butter and the flour in a saucepan. Whisk and cook over medium heat for about 2 minutes. Whisk in the cream, vermouth, V-8 juice, lemon peel, and lemon juice. Bring to a gentle boil, whisking to create a sauce of medium consistency. Set aside.

In a 10-inch skillet, melt the remaining 2 tablespoons butter. Add the mixed vegetables, the sauce, and the shrimp and grouper in that order. Cover with a tight-fitting lid and cook over high heat. Every 30 seconds press the lid tight onto the pan and shake the pan vigorously—*do not lift the pan from the burner.* Steam will begin to escape from the pan in about 7 minutes. Check to see if the grouper is cooked. Do not stir as this will break up the fish chunks. Replace the lid and continue to simmer and shake until just cooked, about 10 minutes in all. Do not worry if the sauce appears to separate; the shaking will fix this.

Divide and gently spoon onto the individual pastry bottoms, top with the pastry lids and serve. **Serves 4.**

(To double this recipe repeat in another 10-inch skillet.)

STONE CRAB SERENADE

A Picnic for Four

Gazpacho
Chunky Cucumber Salad
Beer Bread
Steamed Crab Claws
Mustard Sauce
Lemon Angel Cake

Dixie Beer

"I decided to throw a party, something nice, something with an orchestra, by the sea with food, the tradewinds in the sea grapes...." Chester Hunicutt Pomeroy, the entertainer of Thomas McGuane's *Panama* has the right idea. Outside with music. Breezes and the sound of waves dashing the shore. Jasmine candles and small white lights to mimic the smell and sight of a night beach in the season of phosphorescence.

When the night's hot and a cool breeze seems months away, plan a picnic outside your summer house or on the beach. Choose a color scheme of coral and gray with hints of sea green. Lay out a gray dhurrie rug or bedsheet on the grass or on the sand; place a coral-and-white lacy tablecloth on top of that to add a hint of elegance. Set out large, gray buffet plates, with a delicate, coral patterned plate on top. Fold cloth napkins, incorpo-rating cool-colored pastel fans for each guest into the napkins. You want to emphasize airiness and tasteful informality. Select a number of small, white, jasmine candles for the blanket, placing them randomly on the "table."

If you're outside the house—not on the beach—form a border around two sides of the picnic cloth with potted green plants, and if you really want to splurge, get some flowering jasmine for the centerpiece. Place it off-center in the corner where the potted plants meet.

If picnickers outside the house are within reach of an electrical outlet, rig up some of the littlest white Christmas lights to deco-rate the trees. Conjure up images of the ocean's glow and eat heart-ily. Everything can be prepared in advance, unless you want to eat the crab claws while they're still hot. (You can even make all the food except the crab the day before.)

Fred Lyon/Wheeler Pictures

The flowerpot border works for more elegant picnics as well. Pale geraniums and a white poinsettia balance the fine china and more intricately prepared food (below left). Crab claws lend themselves to informal simplicity. Good bread, wine, a marinated salad, and sauces are the perfect accompaniments to fresh crab (left).

JOE'S STONE CRAB RESTAURANT'S MUSTARD SAUCE

A Miami classic, Joe's Stone Crab Restaurant serves up sea-fresh, scrumptious crabs. Steam the crabs, crack the claws, and serve with this well-known sauce.

3 1/2 teaspoons Coleman's Dry English Mustard
1 cup mayonnaise
2 teaspoons Lea & Perrins Worcestershire sauce
1 teaspoon A-1 Sauce
1/8 cup light cream
1/8 teaspoon salt

Put the English mustard in a mixing bowl, then add the mayonnaise and beat for one minute. Add the remaining ingredients and beat until the mixture reaches a creamy consistency. Chill. **Serves 4**.

Outdoor Illuminations

Adding the right light to a night's festivities can set the mood and serve a practical purpose at the same time. If you're working from a house with an electrical source, you have many more options, but the choices for a beach setting can be just as dramatic or subtle.

Wherever you're setting up, plan to keep the lights low but with enough glow that your guests can see the food and each other. Candlelight is sufficient for the table; there's an array of outdoor candle holders that keep out the wind. For the background, white lights blend in well without distracting guests. Use colors if you want a showy, carnival atmosphere. A set-up of small, one-color Christmas lights can cast a pretty glow.

Make sure, too, that you provide some illumination near or on footpaths, stairs, rocks, and other potentially hazardous areas. These guiding lights should be placed discreetly, with the glimmer filtering through to the appropriate spot. Spotlights or lanterns are better than candles along paths, just in case someone loses his or her balance on the way.

If you have a swimming or reflecting pool (or can dig a small basin of water at the beach), you have a wonderful option: float small votive-type candles in petal saucers, or try floating candles.

Torch lights are handy for the beach, as are battery-powered "candles." One such innovation now comes as a waterproof radio-lantern; others are more simple.

Courtesy of Crate and Barrel

Candles in their own containers allow for easy setup and cleanup. Arranging them in a group provides a more powerful glow without compromising the softness of the light.

HAWAIIAN SOJOURN

A Casually Elegant Supper for Four

Mahimahi with Vin Blanc and Mangoes
Sautéed Yam Slices with Ginger
Green Salad with Basil, Tomatoes, and Jicama
Lime Dressing
Selection of Fruit Sorbets
Macadamia Nut Brittle

Jordan Chardonnay 1983 (California) or Puligny-Montrachet 1983 (France)

Captain James Cook of England first named Hawaii *Owhyhee,* after the fashion of the indigenous people there. As Richard Hough describes in *The Last Voyage of Captain Cook,* when the ship anchored off Maui: "At first it was only small quantities of fish and fruit and roots that the natives brought out, but as soon as Cook made known his wishes, he was answered with extravagant gestures indicating plenty. The next morning more canoes came out, well supplied with breadfruit, plaintains, pigs and fruit of many kinds."

It is just in the past year or so that the bounty of Hawaii is reaching the mainland. *Opah,* or moonfish, and *mahimahi* have made their way to the interior; and kiawe wood from Niihau has appeared on grills in place of hickory or mesquite. Flavorful Samoan crabs and *ahi,* a Hawaiian tuna, haven't hit off-island markets yet, but it's only a matter of time before mainlanders can enjoy a full Hawaiian feast.

This is a summer menu, meant to be eaten with the sun shining and the smell of a salty beach nearby. Drag out the lawn or porch furniture, assemble a seating arrangement that encourages conversation, and keep the frills to a minimum. A bare, weathered wood table is a fitting addition to the decor. Other than that all you really need are baskets and platters laden with food and flowers. Orchid sprays, bougainvillaea, and birds of paradise all make suitable table arrangements, especially if they're off-center and surrounded by a cornucopia of produce.

Fruit, cheeses, and breads or crackers can be in sight for snacks during the day, but as supper approaches, recall them to the kitchen; this meal is fruit-laden and filling.

For beach parties of more than four you may want to arrange a sideboard of flowers, fruits, and other foods. Raise a weathered plank off the sand with rocks or driftwood logs and go from there (right).

Papier-mâché and wooden trays, wicker and straw baskets double as serving dishes and table decor for patio entertaining. Placemats evocative of sea fans highlight the offshore spirit (far right).

Gordon E. Smith

Elizabeth Heyert

THE BATIK ROOM'S MAHIMAHI WITH VIN BLANC AND FRESH MANGOES

Chef Bernd Bree at the Westin Mauna Kea's Batik Room has a reputation that has leapt to the mainland. Make sure the mangoes are ripe before you attempt this recipe; otherwise you'll have wasted your efforts.

1 large mango
4 slices of fresh mahimahi, ³/₄ inch thick and 6 ounces each
Salt and pepper to taste
Juice of 1 lemon
Sprinkling of flour
4 tablespoons butter
1 tablespoon oil
¹/₂ cup white wine
¹/₂ cup fish stock
Coriander leaves for garnish

Peel the mango and cut the fruit away from the seed in long slices. Set aside.

Sprinkle the fish lightly with salt, pepper, and a little lemon juice. Dust with flour. Heat 2 tablespoons of the butter and 1 tablespoon oil in a skillet and lightly sauté the fish for 3 minutes a side. Remove from frying pan. Add the remaining 2 tablespoons butter, white wine, fish stock, and lemon juice to the skillet and cook over high heat until all the ingredients are well reduced and emulsified. Add the mango slices and heat through. Pour sauce over the fish and garnish with the coriander. **Serves 4.**

A Pack of Picnics

Picnics are those rare summer activities that can brighten a day and make even the most hardened cynic into an optimist. Without precaution, however, an ill-planned outdoor meal can send even the heartiest outdoorsman running for the nearest screened-in enclosure. Keep in mind the following tips when organizing your next picnic.

• Make sure all protein and dairy-based foods are kept chilled and away from direct sunlight. A beach umbrella—even if you're on solid ground—can help keep food shaded and relatively cool once you've arrived at your destination.

• If you're going to an area you're unfamiliar with, bring insect repellant, suntan lotion, and, if at all possible, a low table that will discourage ants from spoiling the event.

• Consider setting up a cabana if you're on the beach to keep out unwanted sun and breezes. No matter how delightful the first few hours of sun and wind feel, after a full day's exposure you'll be happy to have some protection. For that matter, make sure you bring a change of clothes, including a sweatshirt or other warm clothing.

• Be aware that sand has a tendency to get into everything, even raised platforms. Accept this and enjoy the meal. The amount of sand that gets into most things will be minimal if you exercise a little care.

• Try to bring all the food pre-prepared. (There will be exceptions, of course, such as some salad dressings.) Put seasonings into small containers (pretty mini-boxes or colorful gift enclosure envelopes can add a festive note, provided they're carefully sealed).

• Last but not least: If you don't know what resources are in your picnic area, bring fresh water for drinking—even if you're serving other beverages.

CALIFORNIA A DEUX

A Romantic Dinner for Two

Chèvre on French Bread with Rosemary
"Boats of Abalone" Monterey
String and Butter Beans Almandine
Coeur à la Creme

Le Flaive Bâtard-Montrachet 1982 (France)
or Roederer Cristal Champagne 1981 (France)

"Monterey sits on the slope of a hill, with a blue bay behind it and with a forest of tall dark pine trees at its back," wrote John Steinbeck in *Tortilla Flat*. The setting is still mysterious and lovely at night, with long drives and equally long vistas out to sea—a perfect milieu for a romantic meal.

The Sardine Factory, a renowned restaurant in Monterey, specializes in one dish well suited for an evening of amour: tartlets of puff pastry filled with abalone and spinach in a rich cream sauce and topped with hollandaise. The garnish of the "boats of abalone"—red peppers—lends color to the sable of the night sky if you're eating outdoors.

Dramatic reds and blacks stand out lustily on the table in the dark of a candlelit night. Set a round table with a boldly designed cloth that reaches to the ground. Add black matte napkins and sterling silver napkin rings, and you have the basic setting. A quartet of black matte porcelain candleholders with white candles brings a distinguished touch of romance to the table, while black and white faux marble service plates inject a little fun. Use smaller black matte dishes to top the service plates, or for a more simple look, use clear glass dishes.

Silver and black porcelain Art Deco and newer, Italian-styled Memphis accessories blend in well in a black-and-red motif. To play up the elegance of the evening include an ice bucket, a woven silver basket, and sleek sterling salt and pepper shakers.

Potted miniature evergreens placed on corners of a patio can bring the outdoors just that much closer, or if you have the vegetation in your backyard, set up the table among the trees and let the stars add to your candle glow.

The most important consideration of the night, however, is to relax and enjoy whatever happens. Prepare the tartlets in advance, finishing the filling just before you sit down to dinner. Put the rest of the meal together as you can; if you don't have a lot of time, substitute a simple store-bought loaf of bread and dessert, and serve green beans dotted with butter and a squeeze of lemon juice.

The soft canopy, bamboo struts, and rattan mat transform this simple patio into a romantic annex bordered by potted fuschias. The candles, off-center, provide supplementary lighting to a spot-light that is mounted (out of view) on the house.

Bill Rothschild/Designer: Nicholas Calder

SARDINE FACTORY'S "BOATS OF ABALONE" MONTEREY

1 pound puff pastry
3 pounds fresh spinach, cooked
3 teaspoons chopped garlic
4 teaspoons chopped shallots
2 teaspoons fresh lemon juice
1 tablespoon white wine
2 pounds, 4 ounces abalone, cut into $1/2$-ounce pieces
24 medium mushrooms, sliced
6 tablespoons whipping cream
1 red bell pepper
1 cup hollandaise sauce

Preheat the oven to 450 degrees. Roll out puff pastry to $1/4$-inch thickness. Cut out squares the size of tartlet pans. Grease the tartlet pans lightly with butter, then press the puff pastry into the pans with your fingers, pressing lightly so the dough is not too thin. Trim excess dough from top of tartlets with a knife. Sauté the cooked spinach in a lightly greased pan with 2 teaspoons of the garlic, 2 teaspoons of the shallots, 1 teaspoon of the lemon juice, and 1 tablespoon white wine until hot. Remove from heat and drain in a strainer to remove excess liquid. Place 4 tablespoons of the mixture into each tartlet. Place three $1/2$-ounce pieces of abalone on top of the spinach, evenly spaced. In a greased skillet, place slice mushrooms, remaining garlic, shallots, lemon juice, white wine, and whipping cream. Let reduce on medium heat until whipping cream becomes thick. Remove from heat and let cool. After cooling, place 3 slices of mushrooms on top of the abalone in each tartlet. Along the sides of the tartlets, place 3-inch strips of red peppers. Place boats of abalone on a baking pan, and bake for approximately 13 minutes. Remove from oven, and turn oven up to 500 degrees. Top boats of abalone with 1 tablespoon of hollandaise and put back in the oven until the hollandaise has turned lightly brown. **Serves 6.**

NORTHWEST INFLUENCE

A Broiled Dinner for Six

Oysters on the Half Shell
Grilled Salmon, Pot Latch Style
Spinach
New Potatoes with Dill
Raspberry, Blueberry, and Blackberry Charlotte
Red Hook Ale

Archambault Sancerre 1985 (France)

This is not a meal for the faint of heart. It smacks of bold adventure matched with flawless tradition. Carry the feeling through to the setting with stylized Beth Forer tableware in white and black, complemented by speckled underplates and flatware; order some spotted arachnis for the centerpiece and set it all down on a black-and-white patterned tablecloth. If it's a birthday or other special occasion, sprinkle gray, red, and silver confetti on top (before you set the plates down). Add candles in glass candlesticks and you're ready.

For a more casual luncheon setting, tone down the colors to taupes and light blues. Keep the speckled flatware but opt for a simple plate that complements a soft-weave tablecloth and matching cloth napkin. Peonies or anemones keep the theme light but bold.

No matter what the table setting, the star of this meal is Joyce Goldstein's grilled salmon flavored with juniper berries. Although her restaurant, Square One, is in San Francisco, she has adapted a long-standing favorite of Washingtonians—the salmon bake—and brought it up to standards to delight any gourmet.

Make the charlotte the night before, so it holds its shape well. While the salmon is marinating, wash the smallest new potatoes you can find and peel them with one stripe down the middle. Sauté them in clarified butter and sprinkle with snipped dill. Have the spinach steaming while you're preparing the potatoes; serve with lemon juice and a hint of butter. Enjoy the oysters with your guests before you put the salmon under the broiler. Then settle in and relax to an extraordinarily simple meal.

Salmon steaks grilled or broiled with just lemon and butter are a simple—but not as special—variation on Square One's recipe with juniper berries. Garnish with lemon slices and dill to dress up the plate.

This lunch setting encourages relaxation and comfort. The colors and soft weave add a casual note, while the place setting itself, including the shells, lends an air of unceremonious decorum.

Gordon E. Smith

SQUARE ONE'S GRILLED SALMON, POT LATCH STYLE

This recipe is simple, tasty, and not overly rich. It can be prepared with a whole side of salmon, skin on. If you choose to use the full side of salmon, first remove all the bones with pliers.

6 salmon fillets, 5 to 6 ounces each (not salmon steaks)
3 tablespoons coarse salt
8 tablespoons sugar
3 teaspoons juniper berries, ground fine in a spice grinder
Freshly ground black pepper, to taste
Oil to brush the fish

The fish may be grilled on an outdoor barbecue or in a home broiler. Combine the salt, sugar, and juniper berries. Add a bit of black pepper. Rub the spice mixture on the fish and let marinate for at least 4 hours but no more than 12 hours.

Brush the fish fillets with oil. Grill 2 to 3 minutes on each side. Serve with a lemon wedge. **Serves 6.**

Randy O'Rourke

MEXICAN SIESTA

A Light Lunch for Two or More

Cold Avocado Soup
Maine Lobster Tacos
Mango Ice

1985 Muscadet Sèvre-et-Maine Guilbaud (France)

"Mexico is a land of color amid great poverty. Traditional Indian costumes are woven in vibrant reds and rich purples; homes painted in shocking pinks...and balloons colored in orange, yellow and fuchsia," write Lynn and Lawrence Foster in *Fielding's Mexico*. The country's cuisine reflects much of its history—a mélange of influences, from the ancient cultures, from Spain, from France, as well as from the United States. Let the blending of peoples and customs guide your hand as you prepare a table setting for this Mexican-inspired meal. This is not a lunch for which you'll set out your best china. Choose, instead, a mixing and matching of colors and textures. Pictured here are two variations on a theme. Both use a subtle range of bright colors to produce a warmth that extends beyond the table into the entire room. Use natural lighting or low lights in the corners of the room (save the candles for a dressier occasion).

An Indian-print tablecloth or an American folk quilt can be just as eye-catching and appropriate as a Mexican blanket for a tablecloth; a simple vase or south-of-the-border earthenware figurine can highlight an arrangement of sunflowers or wildflowers. (Snip a bloom for each place setting or float a blossom on the surface of the soup.)

The center of attention here will be chef Bill Hufferd's Maine Lobster Tacos from Venice, California's West Beach Cafe, a restaurant known for its unusual menu offerings. You can make the salsa, the soup, and the mango ice ahead, leaving the tacos to the last minute. Gather your friends around the barbecue and assign one of them to watch the lobsters while you heat the tortillas; in an instant the meal will come together easily and casually with hardly any effort.

Jeff McNamara (James Goslee III, stylist)

Each element—the overcloth, chairs, floral arrangement, and dishware—affects the full scene. The variations shown here present two casual lunch settings in the same house; changing the elements in each brings out a slightly different mood. Both are relaxed and homey and both incorporate country themes appropriate to the beach house walls. Both emphasize color and texture, yet the one at right encompasses a southwestern/Mexican motif, while the one at left hints at a pastoral nostalgia.

Jeff McNamara (James Goslee III, stylist)

WEST BEACH CAFE'S MAINE LOBSTER TACOS

This intriguing recipe comes not from Maine nor the Mexican coast but from California, from funky, affluent, paradoxical Venice, where canals survive as reminders of their sister town in Italy and where the beach spirit holds sway over much of the population.

4 pink grapefruits
2 fresh serrano chilies
¼ medium purple onion
4 tablespoons coarsely chopped cilantro
1 teaspoon salt
2 Maine lobsters, 1½ pounds each
Fresh tortillas

The Salsa: With a sharp knife remove the sections of grapefruit. Cut the sections into ¼-inch lengths. Cut the serrano chilies in half lengthwise and slice into thin half-moons. Finely chop the purple onion. Combine the grapefruit, onion, chilies, cilantro, and salt to taste. Set aside, draining in a colander.

The Lobsters: Cut the lobsters in half lengthwise. Rinse the body cavities and pull off the claws. Crack the claws with the back of a heavy knife until the shell is well broken. Broil the lobsters and claws in a hot oven, or better yet char them, meat side first, on an outdoor barbecue.

Together: Arrange the lobsters, meat side up, on the serving platter and fill the body cavities with the grapefruit salsa. Arrange the claws around the lobster. Serve with warm tortillas. **Serves 2.**

HEARTY CHINESE

A Sino-American Supper for Four

Hot and Sour Soup
Spring Rolls
Stir-Fried Shrimp with Vegetables
Fried Rice with Tree Ears
Sesame Green Beans
Green Tea and Red Bean Ice Cream
Almond Cookies

Kirin Beer or Hugel Gewürztraminer 1983 (France)

Chinese food has become ubiquitous within the last decade in the United States. A tiny Cantonese restaurant in upstate Wisconsin may not have chopsticks, but it can stir-fry a dish to your heart's desire. Setting the scene for a Sino-American meal need not include Polynesian paper umbrellas and scroll paintings typically found in Chinese restaurants. Use your imagination and retreat to the days of dynastic China "when lords and ladies have their dainty beds and where stand their lacquered boxes of black and red and gold...." (from Pearl Buck's *The Good Earth*).

Find a remnant of rough silk and drape it on the table as a tablecloth. Use a dignified pattern of china that picks up the hues of the material, or black lacquer plates. Scatter a few Chinese boxes around the table, or, if it's a special occasion, place a small, silk-covered box by each setting. For a classic touch, arrange fresh flowers in an antique incense burner. Subdued golds, vermilion, and navy blues are colors to keep in mind.

Use plain white porcelain soup bowls with Asian-style spoons and offer porcelain chopsticks with matching rests for those guests who want them. Traditional meals necessitate a separate rice bowl.

If you choose to stop by a local restaurant to supplement your main dish, this meal can be the perfect solution to entertaining after a long workday. You can buy all the extras or plan to buy everything except the fried rice and green beans. By making these latter two yourself, you have the option of making a simpler fried rice (seasoned with soy sauce, scallions, fried eggs, peas, and tree ears) and a more subtle vegetable accompaniment than many restaurants offer. In either case, if children are about, don't forget the fortune cookies!

Although many patterns of Chinese dinnerware come in time-honored blue and white, selections now include bold red-and-black designs that are inspired by traditional Chinese architecture.

STIR-FRIED SHRIMP WITH VEGETABLES

1 pound medium shrimp
Pinch of kosher salt
1 egg white
1 tablespoon cornstarch
2 teaspoons plus 1 tablespoon Chinese wine or dry sherry
Vegetable oil (preferably soy oil)
Approximately 12 pea pods
1 red bell pepper
2 to 3 garlic cloves
2 scallions
Small coin of ginger
Pinch of red pepper flakes
1 tablespoon soy sauce
1 teaspoon Chinese vinegar
1 teaspoon sugar
1 teaspoon cornstarch dampened with water (optional)

Clean, peel, and devein the shrimp. Place in a shallow bowl and sprinkle with a small amount of kosher salt. Whisk the egg white with the cornstarch and 2 teaspoons wine; whisk in 2 teaspoons of the vegetable oil until combined. Pour the marinade over the shrimp and refrigerate, covered, for at least half an hour.

Rinse the pea pods and pepper and cut into 1-inch pieces. Set aside. Mince the garlic, ginger, and the scallions and set aside. Add the red pepper to the same plate as the garlic mixture.

Heat a wok just until it smokes. Add 1 tablespoon of vegetable oil and heat. Add the shrimp and stir-fry for 1 minute or a little less, until the shellfish turn pink. Take the shrimp out with a slotted spoon or wire-weave wok utensil, and set aside.

Add 1½ tablespoons of vegetable oil to the wok and heat. Add the garlic mixture and hot pepper flakes and stir for about 20 seconds. Put in the pea pods and stir-fry for approximately 2 minutes, or until the vegetables are heated through but still firm. Mix together the 1 tablespoon wine, soy sauce, vinegar, and sugar. Add the cornstarch-water combination for a thicker sauce. Add the shrimp and toss for another minute. Adjust soy sauce for desired saltiness. **Serves 4.**

Variation: Add 4 to 8 ears of canned baby corn and 2 mushrooms, sliced. (If you do this, you may want to keep the pea pods uncut.) Add to the wok when you stir-fry the other vegetables.

Note: Make an effort to use Chinese ingredients; the taste of the finished product will be noticeably different if you do. I've had good luck using shaoshing rice wine, Pearl River Bridge Superior Soy Sauce, and Shinkiany Vinegar. Refer to the Useful Addresses section for companies that will accept mail orders in the United States.

NOD TO THE RISING SUN

Hijiki

Clear Soup with Tofu and Scallions

Sake Scallops

Rice

White Chocolate Mousse in Raspberry Sauce

Sake

To assemble the makings of a true Japanese meal is not so difficult, but to offer a feast with the subtlety and depth of a traditional sit-down dinner, one must understand the philosophy behind the food. Balance and harmony are crucial to the menu. As are bowls and plates works of art.

Rice, soup, and three dishes comprise a standard meal. The soup—whether clear *suimono* or cloudy *miso*—precedes a serving of raw fish, usually *sashimi*, which is the chef's masterpiece. (*Sashimi*, "raw fish," differs from *sushi;* the latter is a piece of raw fish on or rolled up with vinegared rice and a dab of *wasabi*, a hot, green Japanese horseradish.) A grilled or fried dish such as *tempura* or *yakitori* follows, to be followed in turn by a steamed or simmered dish. Pickles and green tea end the meal.

Every course is garnished or presented simply. Black sesame seeds, thin plastic "greenery," tomato roses—each of these is a common adornment to a Japanese meal. But none of them appear in conflict with the dinnerware. The chosen plates are always considered with the specific foods in mind; here they are, again, Japanese-inspired rather than traditional. Made of terra cotta and glazed in patterns that evoke postmodern funk and Orientalia alike, the plates do not detract from the food. The simple glazes in white and blue-green provide a backdrop for the translucent soup and darkened scallops.

The hijiki, a nutritious and flavorful seaweed, can be ordered from specialty shops. For a bit more authenticity, add some pickled ginger to your order. The white chocolate mousse is a departure from the norm, although the thought to color and texture is definitely apparent.

Ceramics by Jane Sachs / Photograph by Sarah Wells

Terra cotta dinnerware in bold, modern shapes takes on a Japanese feel when the color scheme is dominated by black, white, and brown.

THE ARK'S SAKE SCALLOPS

Chef Lucas likes cooking with scallops partly because their texture is so smooth when prepared well and partly because they pick up so well the flavors of her striking sauces.

4 ounces scallops (Oregon or East Coast sea scallops)
Clarified butter for sautéeing
$1/4$ teaspoon garlic, minced
$1/4$ teaspoon chopped fresh ginger
Squeeze of lemon
$1/3$ cup sliced mushrooms
$1/4$ cup sake
4 tablespoons teriyaki sauce
3 slivers bell pepper
$1/4$ cup fresh chopped tomatoes
Orange zest for garnish
Sprig of parsley for garnish

Sauté the scallops in clarified butter; add the garlic, ginger, lemon, and mushrooms. Deglaze with sake. Reduce, adding the teriyaki sauce. If need be, remove the scallops from sauce as it reduces. Scallops must not cook for more than 4 minutes. At end, add the bell pepper and tomatoes. Garnish with orange zest and parsley.

Note: Be prepared before you start cooking, because temperature and time are vital to the quality of scallops.

TERIYAKI SAUCE

4 teaspoons fresh garlic
$1/2$ teaspoon fresh ginger
1 cup soy sauce
$2/3$ cup sherry
Juice of 2 lemons
$1/2$ cup brown sugar
2 to 3 tablespoons honey

For the teriyaki sauce, process the garlic with the ginger. Add the soy, sherry, lemon juice, brown sugar, and honey. Blend. **Recipes are per serving: multiply as needed.**

One of the leaders in modern textile design, Marimekko is known for its bright colors and bold prints, many of which have engendered table accessories such as napkins, dishware, and cutlery.

SCANDINAVIAN SMORGASBORD

Luncheon Buffet for Ten

Pickled Herring
Gravad Lax
Smoked Salmon
Smoked Sable
Poached Cod
Mustard-Dill Sauce
Horseradish Sauce
Chopped Beets
Grated Apples
Lemon Wedges
Capers
Cucumber Salad
Black Bread · Rye Bread

Aquavit or Korbel Brut (California)

To begin with you need bread, butter, and pickled herring. Beyond that you must delve into the depths of Scandinavian cuisine because almost any dish can turn up on a smorgasbord (literally a "bread and butter table"), which is the Swedish equivalent of an American potluck get-together. Some sources suggest that smorgasbords began when church services ran so long that families were missing their afternoon meal; the women then brought food to be shared by all.

This smorgasbord departs from the traditional mix of fish and meat dishes because it focuses on fish—smoked, pickled, sugar-cured, and poached. You'll probably want to buy as much as you can: the herring, the smoked salmon and sable, and even the gravad lax. Poach the salmon (see "Poaching" on page 90) the day of the smorgasbord; it won't take long. The only other preparations will be attending to the sauces, beets, and apples.

Taking a cue from Scandinavian design, the table setting can either stem from a bare wood and wildflower motif or be based on any one of the great Marimekko patterns that have been imported to the United States. Whichever you choose, keep the accessories to a minimum; this is not the meal for which you'll want candles and elaborate centerpieces.

Prepare a buffet table following the order of the menu above. You may also want to set up a side table for drinks.

As an ambitious extra, make rosettes with a dusting of sugar or Swedish limpa (a kind of bread), either of which will add a taste of the "homeland."

Jeff McNamara

Smoked fish plays a prominent role in most smorgasbords. The knife at left in the picture is specifically designed for cutting thin, even slices of this delicacy. The pliers, at top, sit ready to pluck out any bones, if necessary.

GRAVAD LAX

The basic recipe for gravad lax, or gravlax, is simple. Time turns the salmon into a slightly sweet, meltingly smooth treat for the taste buds.   Slice thin with a cold knife and serve.

2 pounds filleted salmon
$^1/_2$ to $^2/_3$ cup chopped fresh dill
$^1/_4$ cup of salt
$^1/_4$ cup of sugar
10 white peppercorns, crushed
$^1/_4$ teaspoon ground allspice

Rinse the salmon and pat dry. Place half the dill in the bottom of a pan large enough to hold the salmon without overlap. Mix the salt, sugar, peppercorns, and allspice and rub into the fish. Turn the fish over, sprinkle with the rest of the dill and spices, then cover with a double layer or double-strength plastic wrap. Place a wooden board on top of the covered fish, then place weights (or unopened cans of food) on top of this. Refrigerate with the weights on for 20 to 24 hours. Drain the fish and remove the spices (*do not rinse*). Slice thin on the diagonal and garnish the plate with dill. **Serves 10.**

SALUT A LA FRANCE

Consommé
Asparagus in Puff Pastry
Sea Bass Wrapped in Lettuce with Lobster Stuffing and
Truffle Sauce
Red-Leaf Lettuce, Arugula, and Pecan Salad
Coffee Soufflé
Assortment of French Chocolates

Château de Mersault 1982 (France) or Corton Charlamagne 1983 (France)

For those who love to eat, *France* is a magical word, a note from the piper's pipe that sets people flocking to follow the great chefs: Paul Bocuse, the Troisgros brothers, Roger Vergé, and many more. French food has become the epitome of elegant dining in the United States. This sea bass dish from Café 43, a treat for the eyes as well as for the palate, continues a tradition of aesthetics that is not taken lightly in its home country—France.

Rudolph Chelminski, the journalist who knows the world of French cooking as well as any American could, writes: "The table in France is so much more than a simple place of nourishment that it must be regarded as a specific national phenomenon and point of cultural identification...." And so the recipe within this section should not be tackled by the faint of heart or by the cook who does not feel exhilerated and comfortable working in the kitchen for hours on end. This is a challenge, with results that delight and intrigue and tempt.

And the trappings for such an undertaking deserve the very best. You may want to call your guests in from the beach wearing sandals and swimsuits, but then again, you may want to encourage more dignified apparel. If you're serving seafood in midwinter, ask your guests to "dress." If you're at the beach, ask your guests to bring one small item to spark people's imaginations: a boa, a rhinestone tiara, a red silk bowtie.

The table setting should equal the dinner as well. Wedgwood's Runnymede Dark Blue is a nineteenth-century pattern with a rich enameled cobalt border highlighted by a coral shell motif. The centerpiece of flowers and shells in shades of spring green, pink, lilac, and grayish blue allows you to mix the accompanying glassware: try to find cameo crystal in colors to match the centerpiece, or set the table with etched crystal. The matching Runnymede napkin rings look best with white or coral linen napkins. Pick up the shell pattern with scallop shell silverware.

Very few dishes lend themselves to seafood meals as well as Wedgwood's Runnymede Dark Blue pattern that highlights a coral-colored scallop shell motif.

The south of France, rich with Mediterranean seafood, gave birth to bouillabaisse and salad Niçoise, among many other fine dishes (right). When boiling or steaming asparagus, simmer gently and be sure not to overcook the stalks as the tender tips will lose their flavor and come apart (below).

The occasion deserves sterling candlesticks and candles to match the hue of the napkins. For the tablecloth, stick with a classic linen of white or taupe.

Plan this meal well, making sure that the soufflé will come out just when it's needed. The undressed salad and consommé can be prepared earlier in the day, and you'll want to take the frozen puff pastry out of the freezer well in advance of dinner time. (Check the manufacturer's directions, if you're using the store-bought kind.) Top the night off with espresso served in demi-tasse cups with a twist of lemon zest. Both bon appétit and bonne nuit are assured with this meal.

CAFÉ 43'S SEA BASS WRAPPED IN LETTUCE WITH LOBSTER STUFFING AND TRUFFLE SAUCE

Chef Patrick Verré was trained in France and worked for Windows on the World and Cellar in the Sky before coming to Café 43. His sea bass wrapped in lettuce is a dish to be presented to those around you who are most special.

2 whole sea bass, 2 pounds each
4 whole Maine lobsters, 1½ pounds each
4 large leaves of greenleaf lettuce
2 tomatoes, peeled, seeded, and julienned as garnish

Fillet the sea bass or have the fish store do it. You should have 4 fillets. Set bones and heads aside. Chill fish.

Make court-bouillon (see page 92) in a large saucepan by sweating the vegetables (onion, celery, and carrot), adding vinegar, white wine, pepper, bay leaf, thyme, chervil, parsley, and 1½ quarts water. Let simmer for 30 minutes.

Remove claws and end piece (as shown in the photograph of the finished dish) from the live lobsters. Poach these in boiling court-bouillon for 3 minutes. Remove the pot from the heat and allow the lobster to cool in the court-bouillon. Remove the claw meat from the shells and set aside.

Separate the lobster tails from the bodies. Remove the raw tail meat from the shells. Chill the meat and set the shells aside while you make the bisque.

BISQUE

6 shallots, chopped
Lobster shells (from above), chopped
2 teaspoons sweet butter
¼ cup Cognac
1 cup white wine
1 quart court-bouillon
Tomato, seeded and chopped
½ cup fresh tarragon leaves
Salt and cayenne pepper to taste

In a large saucepan, sweat the chopped shallots and chopped lobster shells in unsalted butter. When the shells have turned red, flambé with a splash of Cognac and deglaze with white wine. Add the court-bouillon, chopped tomato, and tarragon leaves. Let simmer and reduce until it coats the back of a spoon. Strain through a fine chinois. Season to taste with salt and cayenne pepper. Chill.

The presentation of food on a plate, rooted in traditional French cookery, reached its peak in nouvelle cuisine; the sea bass wrapped in lettuce from Café 43 combines a bit of the old with a bit of the new.

STUFFING

10 ounces fillet of sole
Lobster tail meat (from above)
Lobster coral (if available, from above)
2 ounces lobster bisque (from above)
1¼ cups heavy cream
2 shallots, chopped
1 bunch chives
Salt and pepper to taste

Note: All ingredients must be chilled before preparation.

To make the stuffing, purée the sole and lobster meat (and lobster coral, if available) in a food processor, and remove it to a bowl. Add 2 ounces of cold bisque, a little at a time. Add some heavy cream, minced shallots, and chives to the lobster mixture. Adjust salt and pepper to taste, and keep chilled until ready for use.

TRUFFLE SAUCE

3 shallots, chopped
1 celery rib, chopped
1 leek, white part only, chopped
5 mushrooms, sliced
½ bunch parsley stems
1 tablespoon butter
1 garlic clove, minced
Sea bass bones (from above)
Bouquet garni
Cracked white peppercorns
1 cup Noilly Prat (or other dry vermouth)
1 cup white wine
2 cups heavy cream
Salt and pepper to taste
3 ounces truffles, chopped

In a large saucepan, sweat the shallots, celery, leeks, mushrooms, and parsley stems in butter and a little garlic. Then add the reserved sea bass bones, bouquet garni, and cracked white peppercorns. Deglaze with dry vermouth and white wine. Let reduce by two thirds over high heat. Skim top, add heavy cream, and reduce until it coats the back of a spoon, which is the consistency of your final sauce. Strain through a fine chinois. Add salt and pepper to taste and the chopped truffles. Set aside. When ready to serve the dish, bring the sauce to a boil again and finish with a little softened butter.

To prepare the sea bass, place the fillets in a steamer and cook until they are half done (refer to the Canadian Rule on page 79). Place the stuffing on top of each fillet and finish cooking. Place a large lettuce leaf on top of each fillet and heat for 5 seconds. Remove from the heat and set on a towel to dry. Place the lobster claws in the steamer to be warmed up.

To assemble the dish, place the reheated sauce on the plate. Place the fillet in the center of the plate. Arrange two claws on each plate at one end of the fillet, and the tail piece at the other end. Place four pieces of tomato julienne on each side of the sea bass. **Serves 4.**

ITALIAN TRANSLATION

A Patio Supper for Four

Prosciutto and Melon
Tonno con Vitello
Composed Salad of Mixed Greens, Red and Yellow Peppers
Anchovy Vinaigrette
Fresh Figs and Pomegranate

Chilled Argusto Dolcetto D'Acqui 1982 (Italy)

When Goethe traveled to Italy as a young man, he kept a journal rich in impressions of the flora, fauna, and landscape. Upon reaching Naples and the sea, he described in lush detail the fleshy Indian figs, humble gray-green myrtles, and pomegranates. On the shore, he saw his first starfish and sea urchins, juxtaposed with beach pebbles in lustrous colors of marble, porphyry, jasper, serpentine, quartz, and greenish-blue glass.

Take a leap from February 24, 1787, to the present, to your own table. Evoke those days of Goethe's journeying by setting a table that is at once lush and spare. Playing on this paradox, set the table with jewel-tone glass plates: emerald green, royal blue, burgundy, amber. Use underplates of contrasting colors. Match these with glassware that hints of color—a blue or green stemmed wine glass or an antique tinted cameo glass.

Choose a sky blue, sea green, or ivory cloth for a runner that covers the center of the table along its length. Sprinkle sand on the cloth, being careful not to spill onto the table. Then set starfish and shells on the sand. If you can get myrtle branches from your local florist, set them or another green among low displays of figs and pomegranates. Cut the fruit in two to highlight the still life, and add grapes if you want to drape something over the container.

The bright hues of the table setting call for a dish that has a strong personality of its own. Chef Steven Mellina at the Manhattan Ocean Club has adapted a traditional Italian dish that is the perfect centerpiece for a casually elegant light supper on the patio.

Set up a buffet on the patio. If you have room, set up the side table with the sand-and-shell combination, too. Have the melon and prosciutto, the salad, and the quenelles ready before the guests arrive. The tuna can be prepared in the kitchen and brought to the patio on a tray. This mix of casual and formal is an easy way to entertain friends and let them know how special you think they are. The meal will basically take care of itself, and with the exception of the main dish, you won't have to keep dashing in and out of the kitchen.

When serving a dish such as the tuna, it is important to place the food to create a picture, a visual treat. In this case, as mentioned in the recipe, fan out the pieces of fish and put the quenelles either at the bottom of the fan or on the lower sides of the fan in a semi-circle. Add parsley according to preference.

Tim Street-Porter

For a single-hue variation set white on white: dishes, tablecloth, flowers—even a hammock and chairs.

Deglazing

Deglazing is the term used to describe the first step of preparing a sauce or gravy from pan juices—those from roasted or even sautéed poultry or meat. Most of the fat is carefully poured from the pan and any juices or brown material saved. The pan is then place on the stove, and wine, water, or, in this case, Cognac, is added. The pan is then heated while the bottom is scraped carefully to free any flavorful bits that may be stuck there. In the process of the heating and scraping—the deglazing—the Cognac begins to cook down, the mixture thickens, and a sauce is born—ready to be seasoned, thickened, and served.

Styling with Pieces o' Bait

Whenever you plan a meal, your first and foremost consideration is taste. Beyond that, you want to call aesthetics into play, but you don't want to compromise taste for beauty. Remember one thing: do what you can do best. If you try too hard, you're bound to become frantic and overwrought. This holds for styling as well as entertaining in general. Some people have an artistic eye, which they use to make food look spectacular. Everyone else can keep a clipping file specifically for how chefs and stylists set out fish. Below are a few ideas that you can elaborate on or not, as you wish.

Strips: Use fish-strips, as in the Tonno con Vitello recipe, in a fan shape; form a log-cabin style arrowhead, with vegetables below the tent; or make a star with the strips with a garnish or sauce in the center. (See illustration.) A variation on the last suggestion is to make a fan on either side of a central area. For fish that is to be eaten with chunked food, try making a grid, similar to a tic-tac-toe board; put the middle horizontal strip on top of the vertical strips, the first and third horizontal strips below.

Flakes: There are times when no matter how hard you try, fish will not come off the bone as neatly as you had hoped. If you have large but uneven flakes of fish and plan to sauce them, make a flower petal arrangement, similar to the star in the strips illustration; you can use a small flake to fill in the center space. For dinners when you plan to serve flaked fish and have a lot, shape the pieces to resemble the body portion of a fish; poach a fish head and tail and use at either end of the shaped fish and garnish.

THE MANHATTAN OCEAN CLUB'S TONNO CON VITELLO

Fans of Italian cuisine know the popular dish Vitello Tonnato—cold roast fillet of veal with tuna sauce. At the Manhattan Ocean Club chef Steven Mellina has taken this classic dish and reversed it, making it the restaurant's trademark recipe.

1 Bluefin tuna steak, about 1 pound and 2 inches thick
Salt and freshly ground black pepper

Char tuna in a red-hot skillet, quickly blackening the outside, with the inside remaining raw to rare. Season with salt and pepper to taste. Slice into 1/8-inch strips. Fan out on a plate, dividing portions among the guests.

Then, with two tablespoons, form quenelles of vitello paste and place next to the tuna. Garlic croutons are optional. **Serves 4.**

Vitello Paste:
6 ounces veal
Salt and pepper to taste
1 tablespoon butter
Cognac for deglazing
1 1/2 cups mayonnaise
1 anchovy fillet
2 tablespoons capers
1 tablespoon caper juice
1 teaspoon chopped chives
1 teaspoon chopped parsley
1 teaspoon chopped fresh tarragon
Juice of 1/2 lemon

Sauté the veal, seasoned with salt and pepper, in butter until medium to well done. Deglaze with Cognac. Let cool. In a food processor, pureé the cool sautéed veal with mayonnaise and anchovy. Run until smooth. Remove and place in a mixing bowl. Fold in the capers, caper juice, chives, parsley, tarragon, and lemon juice. Season to taste with salt and pepper. The paste is now ready to be formed into quenelles.

Although modern shipping practices allow us to receive fresh fish from all over the world, the initial step in many cases is still in the hands of individual fishermen.

Bring the jewel tones down to the beach in the form of heavy-duty, translucent plastic dishes, tumblers, and cutlery. Pack it all up in a multicolored cotton coverlet along with a few bottles of Italian sparkling water and a handsome homemade bread.

Elyse Lewin (Kim Freeman, stylist)

The influence of Spanish food has crept into the United States without the notice it readily deserves. Through the tapas craze and the new look at South American cuisine, Spanish cookery is gaining recognition. Paella, perhaps the best-known dish, offers a good starting point for exploration.

Bill DeNeergaard

A TASTE OF SPAIN

A Casual Dinner for Six

Paella with Lobster
Flower of Vegetables
Flan
Fresh Orange Sections

Marqués de Cáceres (red) 1982 (Spain) or Viña Morgana Tinto 1980 (Spain)

The White Coast. The Coast of Orange Blossoms. The Land of Rice. All of these names refer to the Levante, the area that begat paella—a rice-based mélange of seafood and chicken redolent of saffron and olive oil. The dish, which began as a simple concoction of rice, snails, eels, and green beans, has come a long way. All paellas include rice, saffron, and fresh food from the market, but now most combine chicken, shrimp, and sausage with fresh vegetables.

Because the origins of this well-known treat are humble, set a table that is comfortable and inviting, with grays and blues that fight for attention with the reds, yellows, and greens of the food. Although you probably won't want to cook the paella outside over a stick-wood fire as the peasants in Spain did, you may want to eat outside. Bring pillows and a rattan mat down to the sand—and a squat table if you have one. A paella pan welcomes family dining in its truest sense—everyone eats out of a central dish—but you'll most likely want to serve the delicacy on individual plates. Keep the paella in the center of the table though, for your guests to pass and dip into at their request.

Preparing this meal can be fun; you may want your guests around—and watching—as the meal comes together from its varied ingredients. Even children can help make the flower of vegetables. Char two red peppers over a flame until their skins turn black; pop them into a paper bag, close the bag, and shake for a minute or two. The skin will peel away from the meat of the pepper easily. Cut the red pepper into long "petals" and alternate with washed pieces of kale that will serve as decoration. Cook until tender at least two spears of asparagus per person and lay them down on the petals of red pepper. Stuff mushroom caps with a béchamel and cheese filling and broil; when still hot, place them in the center of the "flower."

Buy a good, hearty bread from the bakery and serve with tubs of sweet butter and garlic butter. Finish the meal off with flan and offer orange sections (either plain or macerated in Grand Marnier).

TORREMOLINOS' PAELLA WITH LOBSTER

There are almost as many recipes for paella as there are chefs who know how to cook this delicious, extravagant dish. This one hails from one of New York City's best-known Spanish restaurants.

6 clams
6 mussels
2 tablespoons white wine
2 pounds chicken
5 tablespoons olive oil
1 onion, chopped
2 peeled and chopped tomatoes
1/4 pound smoked ham, cut into strips (or pork meat or sausage)
Salt and freshly ground pepper
1 1/2 cups short-grain rice
1/2 cup sliced green beans
3 1/2 cups chicken stock
Pinch of saffron
2 lobsters, 1 pound each
1/2 pound uncooked shrimp
Red pepper strips for garnish
4 ounces artichoke hearts
Asparagus for garnish

Steam the clams and mussels with the white wine in a covered pot for about 10 minutes, or until shells open. Set aside, reserving the juice. Cut up the chicken and brown lightly in 2 or 3 tablespoons of olive oil. Set aside. Sauté the onion in the same pan until transparent; add the chopped tomatoes, smoked ham, and salt and pepper. Return chicken to the pan and simmer 10 minutes.

In another pan fry the rice in 2 tablespoons olive oil until rice begins to toast. Transfer chicken and tomatoes to a paella pan, either metal or earthenware. Add the rice and the sliced green beans. Heat the chicken stock and add a pinch of saffron to the stock. Add the juice from the clams and pour over the mixture. Stir and simmer for 15 minutes (if you have a metal pan, cook it on top of the stove; if it's earthenware, place it in a moderate oven at 375 degrees). Add a few pieces of lobster.

Arrange the uncooked, peeled shrimps, clams, and mussels over the top and garnish with strips of red pepper and cooked artichoke hearts. Cook in 375 degree oven for 15 minutes. The liquid should be absorbed; add more during cooking if necessary. Add asparagus. **Serves 6.**

Take a hint from the Spanish peasants of yore and eat paella outdoors around a central dish. The raised table helps keep out sand and the pillows bring additional comfort to the hard beach.

Jeff McNamara (James Goslee III, stylist)

SHADES OF MOROCCO

A Colorful Lunch for Eight

Minced Lamb in Puff Pastry
Brochettes of Shrimp with Vegetables
Couscous
Orange Salad
Flatbread
Iced Mint Tea
Gingersnaps

Mâcon-Lugny Genevières Louis Latour 1985 (France)

The riches of Morocco became revealed in 1415 when, according to Daniel J. Boorstin in *The Discoverers*, the Portuguese stormed the city of Ceuta. "The loot in Ceuta was the freight delivered by caravans that had been arriving there from Saharan Africa in the south and from the Indies in the east. In addition to the prosaic essentials of life—wheat, rice, and salt—the Portuguese found exotic stores of pepper, cinnamon, cloves, ginger, and other spices. Ceutan houses were hung with rich tapestries and carpeted with Oriental rugs. All in addition to the usual booty of gold and silver and jewels."

With descriptions such as this it's easy to imagine a Moroccan decor adapted American-style. Start with a color scheme that's borrowed from the colors in the market: rich reds, burnt oranges, soft golds.

For real drama, set up a white or golden canopy outside large enough to protect a table for eight. Lay down Oriental rugs beneath the table and by the en-

trance to the canopy. For the tablecloth, find one with an Oriental-inspired weave. Select place mats in a cotton weave and choose an array of colors that will bring out the gold/orange/brick red hues of the rugs. Place a hammered brass bowl filled with dried fruits and whole nuts in the center of the table for the centerpiece. As a final touch, add a brass candelabra with honey-colored candles.

For a different look—one that may evoke stretches of unmarred Moroccan beach—use rattan and white canvas: place a white canvas cloth on the table, then top with rattan place mats (leaf-shaped or rectangular). Use madras cloth for napkins and a woven basket as a centerpiece. If you're eating outside, fill the basket with fruit and nuts; if you're lunching inside, fill it with a low arrangement of pincushion protea, painted asters, or acacia.

You may want to set up the table or canopy the day before, which is also a good time to pre-

This Moroccan market should pique the imagination, offering ideas for many table settings—from the material hanging on the walls to the colors of the spices.

pare the lamb in puff pastry (if you're really ambitious, try making a tagine from one of Paula Wolfert's cookbooks). The orange salad flavored with purple onions should be assembled a few hours before the meal as should the tea and the marinade for the brochettes. Save the couscous for last.

If you haven't set up a canopy, you can still inject a bit of the unusual by providing a madras-covered pillow for each armchair at the dining table. Guests can recline in between courses—at the very least, they'll feel the specialness of the meal.

BROCHETTES OF SHRIMP WITH VEGETABLES

2½ pounds small, raw shrimp
1 cup cider vinegar
½ cup safflower oil
4 garlic cloves
¼ teaspoon cumin powder
¼ teaspoon ground ginger (or more to taste)
8 lemon slices
2 red bell peppers
2 green bell peppers
2 Spanish onions
24 small mushrooms

Peel and devein the shrimp and set aside. Whisk the vinegar and oil together, then add the garlic, cumin, and ginger. Add the lemon slices once the marinade is well combined. Put the cleaned shrimp in the marinade, cover, and let sit in the refrigerator for at least 2 hours. Add the vegetables to the marinade about a half hour before grilling. Drain the shrimp, saving the marinade.

Prepare the skewers, each with alternating pieces of shrimp, red pepper, onion, green pepper, and mushroom. Grill over hot coals, basting occasionally with the marinade. **Serves 8.**

Variation: For a more tropical version, omit the cumin and garlic from the marinade and add ¼ cup fresh dill. When preparing the skewers, add chunks of fresh pineapple and sprigs of dill (do not marinate either). You can also substitute scallops for the shrimp or combine the two.

A creative, open mind is also what's needed when serving brochettes: mix ingredients using what's shown here plus onions, squash, plantain, and whatever's fresh and firm in the market.

Dining while sitting on couches or large pillows has become a Moroccan-American standard. Muslin or Haitian cotton provides a cool backdrop that evokes a hot tropical or desert feeling.

Jeff McNamara (James Goslee III, stylist)

THE PERFECT MEAL

Steamed Chilled Lobsters
Kirby Cucumbers
Fresh Berries
Champagne

Wonder it is to see in diverse minds
How diversely Love doth his pageants play,
And shows his power in variable kinds....
—Edmund Spenser
The Faerie Queen

For me to write of *the* perfect meal is to assume a certain hubris, so this is *my* perfect meal. Simplicity, comfort, elegance, and magic unite in a tacitly romantic moment. The sun is setting, sending fingers of color onto low-lying clouds. The senses are exposed: you can hear the waves, feel the mist in the evening air, and smell the change in the tide.

A sandy clearing in the sea grass serves as the table; the cloth, a woven blend of cashmere and wool, cushions the yielding sand. The pillows, trimmed with eyelet lace, lie plumped yet untouched.

The scattered candles, each in a ribbed container, complement the ambient light and give a richness to summer food: crisp cucumbers, juicy native peaches, sweet grapes, fresh whole berries, a ripe Brie, soft and crusty bread. And lobster, steamed then chilled.

Take the ordinary and make it uncommon. Roll a linen napkin into a scroll and tie it with a wide black velvet ribbon. The rolled napkin can easily conceal a small present if that fits in with the day's events. Slender stemmed flutes seem even more delicate when placed against the outdoor backdrop; don't leave them out! Pack them next to the china dishes and bring all in a twig basket which, once emptied, will blend into the scenery.

Elyse Lewin (Kim Freeman, stylist)

Jeff McNamara

CAVIAR

Anytime, Anyplace

Perhaps there is hope for peace between the Soviet Union and the United States; if our political leaders would acquire a true taste for fresh, delicate caviar, they might extend their hospitality into the realm of superpower summits. According to *Cook's* magazine, approximately ninety percent of the "world's premier caviar" comes from the U.S.S.R. Much of the rest is produced in Iran and now in the U.S.

Called the "pearls of the Caspian," caviar—defined as sturgeon roe—was once taken from sturgeon that swam the Hudson, the Po, and the North Sea. Yet the delicacy from the Caspian has always been considered the most sought after. The take of golden caviar, which has never really been available commercially, used to be split between the tsar of Russia and the Persian shah. The rest of us must be happy with osetra (also called ossetra or oestrova), beluga, sevruga, and keluga.

Beluga: Often considered the most-prized caviar, beluga has the largest eggs and comes from the largest of all the sturgeons. The grains, or berries, range from dark to pale gray, the lightest of which are the rarest.

Osetra: The roe of this fish more often than not is a tawny topaz color. The size of the grains falls between that of the beluga and the sevruga. Some connoisseurs prefer the osetra over the beluga because it has a slightly more powerful taste.

Sevruga: The smallest of the three main sturgeon species, sevruga is known for its small, dark eggs—light gray to black. This is the most plentiful of all the sturgeon species, and the one that matures most quickly.

Keluga: The newest caviar to hit the American market, Chinese keluga is reportedly similar to the Russian caviars in texture. I haven't sampled it yet, but it is available through California Sunshine Fine Foods, Inc. in San Francisco.

American Caviar: Most tasters with an experienced palate place American caviar on equal grounds with the mid-quality osetra or sevruga roe, but batches differ from one to another so it's hard to generalize. The texture tends to be slightly more mushy than the imported caviars.

Pressed Caviar: Usually a mix of sevruga and osetra, pressed caviar is made from overripe or damaged eggs. Caviar Direct, a mail-order company based in New York, writes that "up to five times the amount of roe may go into a quantity of pressed caviar,

Judd Pilossof

Gordon E. Smith

giving it unmatched intensity and richness of flavor." Mimi Sheraton has admitted to a preference for this jam-like caviar spread also known as paiusnaya.

Other Caviars: Salmon and lumpfish roe are increasingly seen in containers labeled *caviar.* The large red eggs of the salmon work well as garnish for omelets, pasta dishes, and the like, but should never be cooked; it can also be eaten as you would eat sturgeon roe. Lumpfish caviar, usually dyed bright red or deep black is most useful in canapés with hard-boiled eggs and cream cheese or onion. Note that the dye can run when placed next to moist dairy products. The lumpfish caviar is pasteurized and thus is more salty.

Saltiness, a quality many people dislike in caviar, results from the salt being used as a preservative. The fresher and higher quality caviar—called *malossol,* which means "lightly salted"—is the best.

Serve the gems with buckwheat or plain wheat blinis and crème fraiche. Or place in the center of an ice ring or in a caviar présentoire (Petrossian offers a sterling silver service with a Cristofle glass insert). If you're using an ice ring, make a layer of lettuce leaves beneath the caviar. Then encourage your guests to eat the eggs "neat" with toast spread with just a dab of unsalted butter and sprinkled with a light squeeze from a fresh lemon.

CHAPTER TWO

FISH FACTS

BUYING SEAFOOD

As consumers become more and more aware of the fish market, they are becoming better educated. Nevertheless, it is still common to hear people reject the idea of cooking fish because they don't know how to determine freshness or how to decide which fish is best for which cooking methods (for information on the latter, see Chapter Three). As with any skill, cooking fish requires practice and refinement. The basics, however, can easily be acquired by observing and asking questions.

Market Terms

You can easily get by at the fish market by pointing at a displayed fish, but it's even easier to adopt a certain amount of market jargon. That way, you can ask for seafood that may be in the back of the store and you can make specific requests knowing exactly what you will be getting. Fish are prepared at the market in the following ways:

Whole fish, as it is used in the market, describes a whole fish that has been eviscerated, scaled, and split. A *whole dressed* fish usually means the same thing; the backbone may or may not have been removed. (If you plan to stuff the fish, make sure the fishmonger knows you want the backbone removed.)

Drawn is a term that signifies a small-size whole fish that has had its entrails removed.

Pan-dressed fish can sometimes mean a small fish that, like a whole fish, is eviscerated, scaled, and split. In other places the same term can define a drawn fish. In either case, if you want to use a bigger fish that is a pound or a little over, the head and tail may be removed.

Steaks are cross sections of large dressed fish, usually with part of the backbone attached.

Fillets are the side meat portions of dressed fish that have been cut lengthwise and away from the backbone. Most fillets are virtually boneless. Two fillets connected by skin are called *butterfly fillets*.

What's Fresh and What Isn't

When you're buying fish whole, there are a number of tests for freshness; judge a fish on the basis of all the tests not just one. In time, you'll come to know which markets you can trust, which will make shopping easier. Follow the checklist below to determine freshness:

- The *eyes* should be bright, clear, and bulging. If the fish isn't fresh, the eyes protrude less and are cloudy.

- The fresher the fish, the more reddish-pink the *gills*. No slime or odor should be noticeable.

- The *scales* should adhere to the skin, which should be shiny.

- When pressed with your finger, the fish *meat* should be firm and return to its original shape.
- The fish *odor* should be mild and ocean-fresh not "fishy" or rancid.

When buying fillets, trust your sense of sight. Look at the edges of the fish. If they do not appear to be brown and dry, the fillet is most likely freshly cut.

The guidelines for selecting fresh shellfish differ from those for finfish.

- Live *crab* and *lobsters* should be active or on ice. When crabs are on ice, they should still move at least a bit when nudged. (Lobsters in the tank are acceptable if they are not excessively overcrowded.) No ammonia smell or slime should be present.
- If *clams* are open, have broken shells, or float, discard them. Hard-shell clams, writes Ruth Spear, should have "fine-textured, concrete gray shells that when tapped sound full and solid."
- *Oysters* should not be sluggish when handled. If they are and do not close right away, or if their shells are broken, discard them.
- *Mussels* should close when placed in the freezer for 2 or 3 minutes. Throw away the ones that remain open and any that have broken shells.
- Make sure that *scallops* have a sweet smell and are not crisply dry on the edges.
- Raw *shrimp* should be relatively dry and firm.

How Much Is Just Right?

How much fish to buy depends on how hungry you are. Determining the size of each serving is a perpetually problematic issue. Standards change over the years, as do the trends for serving small, large, or in-between size meals. Any given recipe also influences how much you should buy. With this in mind, use the recommended guidelines for per person amounts. Medium-size servings are assumed unless noted.

Fred Lyon/Wheeler Pictures

FINFISH

Many times when cooking fish, you will choose not to follow a recipe that states an exact amount. Instead, you may simply broil or poach a fish and add an easy sauce on the side. In these cases, figure on $1/2$ pound per person for fillets and steaks; if adding a filling, that amount will be fine for three people. A $1/2$-pound serving is also appropriate for pan-dressed fish, although if you're using drawn fish, plan for $3/4$ pound per person. A pound per person is a satisfactory amount when serving whole fish. If you can, ask the fish dealer how much to get for the number of people being served, because some fish have an unusually large head or other distinctive feature that makes an exception to the rule.

CLAMS

When serving clams raw on the half shell as an appetizer, plan on 6 to 8 per person. For steamers you'll want more, between 1 pint (2 cups) and 1 quart (4 cups) per person, depending on what else you'll be serving. For a general recipe, between 10 and 15 shucked clams is a good but not hearty amount for each diner.

CRABS

Allow 2 or 3 soft-shell crabs or 6 or 7 hard-shell crabs per person. If you're buying the meat only, get approximately $1/4$ pound per person.

Manuel Dos Possos

LOBSTER

A 1- to 1-¹/₂-pound lobster makes a delightful light meal for one person. If you are feeding a hungry gourmand, increase the amount by buying another small lobster rather than buying a 2- or 3-pounder. The larger crustaceans have tougher meat. For recipes that call for meat alone, using ¹/₂ pound per person is a generous but not overbearing amount.

MUSSELS

Mussels have the reputation for being an inexpensive shellfish—and it's easy to gather many containers full with relative ease—so it's not unusual for people to offer generous amounts. (Check with the local tourism office or sports store for areas of untainted shellfish.) About 15 to 20 mussels in the shell make a pound; 25 to 30, a quart. A pint or a dozen mussels in the shell should feed one person easily. If you're buying shucked meat, figure ¹/₂ pound for each person.

OYSTERS

Sizing oysters is not an orderly system as it is with shrimp, so it is hard to say exactly how many are suitable per person. The tiny Olympia oysters are dwarfed by the larger Belons and Malpeques. In general, however, for all oysters but the Olympias, you can assume that 6 to 12 is ample for serving them raw on the half shell. For most appetizers, 4 to 6 is not an unusual number. If you're buying already shucked oysters by the quart, figure on ¹/₄ pint per person or a little more for a generous main dish.

Fred Lyon/Wheeler Pictures

SCALLOPS

Both bay and sea scallops are sold by the pound, so a separate distinction is not necessary. Allot approximately ¹/₃ pound for an appetizer and ¹/₂ pound for a main dish for one person.

SHRIMP

Because these decapods come in a variety of sizes, amounts for shrimp vary widely. Fish markets sell them without the heads as standard practice, so if you see that the ingredients list shrimp tails, you can rest assured that what the fishmonger gave you was correct. In fact, shrimp are sold according to the number of tails per pound. About 15 *jumbo* shrimp make up 1 pound; *large* shrimp come in at approximately 20 per pound; and *medium*, about 30 per pound. A pound of the smallest commercial grade, sold in the shell, yields between 35 and 40 or more shrimp. These *small* shrimp are best for salads and recipes in which the shrimp will be cut up or processed.

Prawns—which look like large shrimp—are often sold as shrimp even though they are not officially and biologically classed as such. The term designates the largest shrimp available on the market.

When buying shrimp, make note that shelling and shrinkage from cooking will reduce the overall weight of meat. Figure on ¹/₂ pound or 12 medium-size shrimp person for a main course, half that for a small appetizer.

Fresh from Your Freezer

Having fresh fish to cook can be an unmatched treat, but sometimes it is necessary to use store-bought frozen seafood. The taste and texture will suffer a little, but, if handled properly, the results are not bad at all.

Judd Pilossof

BUYING, STORING, AND COOKING FROZEN FISH

When buying frozen fish, make sure the package is wrapped well and the meat is frozen through. Freezer burn, which you want to avoid, will show up as white patches on the flesh of the fish. Once the package has been opened, the fish should not give off an offensive smell, nor should it feel cottony; the former indicates spoilage, the latter that the fish has been frozen and refrozen. *Never use fish that has been frozen twice.*

Don't rewrap frozen fish to store it in the freezer; the original packing is suitable. Defrost the fish on the coldest (usually the bottommost) shelf of your refrigerator overnight. Alternatives to this method produce an inferior quality ready-to-cook fish.

When planning to cook frozen fish, allow time for it to be defrosted. If you fry, broil, or bake fish in its frozen state, the results will be disappointing.

STORING FRESH FISH

Often there will be a lag between the time you've made your purchase and the appointed cooking hour. To keep your store "catch" as fresh as possible, rinse the fish in cold water, pat it dry, and wrap it in plastic wrap with a cover of aluminum foil; then refrigerate. Don't keep the fish for more than two days. If you've bought smoked fish, make sure that the wrapping is well sealed. Smoking does not preserve the fish, so use it within three days.

Jeff McNamara

UTENSILS AND COOKWARE

Entering a kitchen supply store can be a dream or a nightmare, depending on your orientation. So many items, all intended to make life in the kitchen easier, bill themselves as *essentials* for the true chef. It becomes confusing all too quickly, especially when you're trying to stock a kitchen for the first time. Even when you have one specific focus—seafood cookery—the choices outnumber what may be practical for you. This chapter functions as a gallery of sorts, a brief look at what utensils and cookware are made especially for cooking fish and shellfish.

Most of the products listed are helpful to have but not all are crucial; a good cook can improvise if need be. Devising new ways to deal with a situation, however, may take more time and be somewhat more problematic. When trying to decide what to buy, consider what you have and how often you expect to make a certain dish. You certainly don't need a fish poacher when you have a covered skillet and you don't often serve poached fish; you can make do with what you already own.

Certain basics are not included here because they are multipurpose pieces. A good baking dish, saucepans, skillets, and a sauteuse fall into this category as do spatulas, slotted spoons, and the like. (For stocking your kitchen with basics, refer to *Pierre Franey's Kitchen* [A Fawcett Columbine Book, 1982], a guide to kitchen equipment including recipes and helpful hints.)

Jeff McNamara (James Goslee III, stylist)

Fish Scalers

The most common fish scaler is a very simple one-piece tool of stainless steel. Standard size is 9¼ inches long with a 4-inch handle. The serrated teeth curve upward so as not to cut into the fish skin as you stroke the scaler against the growth of the scales. *The Cook's Catalogue* (Harper & Row, 1975) includes mention of an aluminum scaler with a hood of sorts that catches the scales for easy cleanup. Although this offers a distinct advantage, it is not as efficient as the more simple scaler, especially when working around the head and the tail.

Fish Knives

There's an assortment of knives to choose from for filleting, cutting, or skinning fish. If you want to use one knife to tackle many chores, use one of the all-purpose wonders that comes complete with a serrated edge for scaling and a scimitar-shaped tip for slitting skin and opening mollusks. The disadvantage to these is control; because they are designed to fit many uses, they lack the ability to do one job with extraordinary ease.

Fillet knives come in a variety of sizes. Most measure between 6 and 12 inches with a relatively narrow blade (although not as narrow as a smoked salmon knife) that tapers to a sharp, even tip; beginners typically start with a 7- or 8-inch blade of stainless steel. These knives are flexible enough to allow the tip to work around the backbone of the fish without giving so much that the movements aren't precise. Becoming proficient with any fish knife is the key to presenting a beautiful dish—a fish with no gashes, or a whole fillet rather than a plate full of small flakes.

Another handy knife to have for preparing larger fish and lobster is a heavy-bladed, 12-inch version of a cook's knife. The blade at the handle usually measures about 3 inches wide. These knives, which are fairly expensive, sever backbones and shells easily. A less expensive alternative preferred by some is a standard Chinese cleaver, which does the job in record time.

For smoked salmon aficionados who buy the whole fish or smoke their own, a very thin slicing knife is necessary. The thin, flexible blade, commonly blunt-tipped, is 12 inches long and most are made of stainless steel.

Fish Scissors

Scissors are an overall kitchen tool that many people overlook. Not only are they good to have on hand for snipping chives and cutting the tops off bacon packages, but they also play a more serious role in fish cookery. Scissors make the job of trimming a fish quick and easy—cutting around gills, removing fins, head, tail, and more. Measured from handle to point, they generally come in three sizes—8 inch, 10 inch, and 12 inch—with slightly serrated edges. Make sure that they are sturdy and well bolted. The blades should fit together perfectly with no visible separation.

Clam Shuckers

These tools are indispensable for anyone who loves raw clams. It doesn't seem to matter whether the handle is rounded or rectangular, polypropylene or beechwood, the all-important factor in choosing a clam knife is comfort. Does it fit into your hand easily? Does it feel good? That is the only real assessment you'll have to make besides one of basic aesthetics—do you prefer a plastic to a wood handle? In general, you'll want to choose a rigid, 3½-inch stainless-steel blade with a rounded tip for cherrystones or clams with a relatively soft shell. A narrow blade with a pointed tip is best for littlenecks or clams with a harder shell.

The advantage of using a knife is that you can direct the juices; you can open the clams over a bowl and save the liquor. If you use a shucking "machine" that sits on the table and has a blunt blade that you pull down onto the clam, you'll lose the precious liquid.

Oyster Shuckers

A typical oyster knife is an unusual-looking utensil. The blade is shaped like an imperfect arrowhead that has been squashed down a bit. At the base of the blade is a shield that protects against accidentally stabbing the hand that holds the oyster. The point, which is rounded on one side and straight on the other, helps in the initial attack on the mollusk. Double-edged blades on some oyster knives make them usable for both left-handed and right-handed people.

Some oyster knives are a little more simple and resemble clam knives with their straight handles and beveled or plain blades with no guard. The lengths of the blades fall between what is usual for a clam knife and for an "arrowhead" oyster knife approximately 3 inches.

A rubber mitt made especially for oyster shuckers hit the market recently. The rubber on the inside of the palm is textured to make a nonslip surface. Both right-handed and left-handed versions are available. For cautious traditionalists, try a cotton or rubber glove.

Sandra Dos Possos

Scallop Knives

Most people buy their scallops already shucked, because this delicate sea creature's shell has openings that allow air in, which quickly dries out the meat; fishermen respond to this by shelling and cleaning the scallops on the boat. A lucky few, however, gather their own scallops, and for these people there are knives made especially for opening both sea and bay varieties. The former are slender and have a curve that follows the shape of the inside of a scallop shell; the latter look very much like rounded-blade clam knives.

Shrimp Deveiners

If you plan to serve shrimp that has not yet been cleaned, a deveiner will become one of your favorite utensils. These fascinating instruments, which come in a variety of shapes and styles, are all designed to make short work of the loathsome task of shelling and cleaning shrimp—either before or after they've been cooked. Inexpensive, the gadgets usually are made of stainless steel or heavy-duty plastic.

Crab Knife

I have yet to see anyone use a crab knife, but *The Cook's Catalogue* writes of one that seems to be designed with sense and knowledge of the task at hand. The 6-inch long "forged and hardened" stainless-steel knife functions in many ways: "A sharp thwack with the heavy handle will crack open the body and claws of the toughest crab, and you can neatly exise the meat from the cracked shells with the short, pointed blade." It also recommends using the blade to kill the crabs before you cook them.

Courtesy of Crate and Barrel

Courtesy of Hammacher Schlemmer

Lobster Utensils

My favorite lobster cracker was recently listed in a catalog that described it as 5½ inches long and "nickel tumbled." This ungainly apparatus is V-shaped and very plain, with ridged inner edges leading up to the vee and spiral pattern around the "handle" area. Its appeal lies in its straightforward functionality. Place a lobster claw, nut, or whatever in the inner ridged area at the join of the vee, then bring the two handles together.

All lobster crackers function in the same way, but there are many designs. Choose crackers on the basis of visual appeal and practicality. If you can, try one on a small nut before you commit yourself to a full set. Many come with lobster picks—also called nut picks—and some with small forks specifically designed for picking meat out of lobster.

Lobsters have also inspired inventors to create beautifully designed pincers whose sole purpose is to make eating this crustacean a pleasure. Of French origin, the stainless-steel gadget is 7⅜ inches long and resembles jewelers' pliers—long, slender, and sleek. The tip is slightly upturned, the grip arced into a graceful elongated oval. Paired with its mate, a pick of polished stainless steel that looks like a chemist's tweezers, the pincers turn eating lobster into a neat and tidy affair.

Poachers and Steamers

Tinned steel and stainless steel are the most practical choices for poachers and steamers; avoid aluminum, which will react badly with acidulated water or other acidic poaching liquids. Look, too, for welded handles. These, in comparison to a bail handle, are better suited to carrying a heavy load of water and fish. A bail handle has a tendency to swing, which, if the poacher contains hot water, could easily cause a messy and potentially painful accident.

Most poachers come in a variety of sizes from about 15 inches all the way up to 36 inches long. You can choose from three shapes, the most common of which—and the traditional version—is a rounded-edge rectangle. Oval shapes are now also available as well as diamond-shape poachers made specifically for turbot. This last pot is more common in Europe than in the United States and has earned its own name there: a *turbotière*.

If you want to use your poacher for company it may be wisest to invest in a mid-size vessel, one that will hold two small fish or one rather large one. Be careful, however, that the poacher isn't too big for a standard-size stove.

Stockpots

When buying a stockpot, consider size, material, and shape. Most likely, you'll opt for an 8- to 12-quart (or larger) pot, because when making stock you may as well make as much as you can and freeze what you don't

need right away. As to material, remember that the hot water will be conducting the heat, so you don't need copper. Stainless steel, aluminum, or a combination of the two are your best bets. Again, because of the conductivity of the water you won't need heavy gauge metal, but you should look for pots that are a little thicker on the bottom so the ingredients don't scorch or burn. Make sure, too, that the pot is taller than it is wide; the narrowness and height keep evaporation to a minimum and allow the liquid to bubble up through the ingredients making the stock all the more flavorful.

If you don't mind spending a little more, you can buy a stockpot with a spigot placed fairly low in the bowl. This allows you to drain off the clear liquid without having to fuss with skimming the fat off the top. Although it minimizes a certain amount of work, the spigot is a luxury that most of us can do without.

If you plan to use the stockpot specifically for aspics, steamed clams or lobsters, or chowders, keep in mind the following. For aspics, you'll want a pot that does not react with acidulated water, so try an enameled steel pot. For steamed shellfish, you'll want the tall and narrow shape as well as a basket or inner, perforated pot. Enameled steel will do well here, too, if you want to produce clear broth. And remember to look for a tight-fitting cover. Clam and fish chowders necessitate a slightly shorter and wider shape, because you'll want to stir the ingredients more often.

Courtesy of Crate and Barrel

Sauté Pans

The phrase "sauté pans," as used here, is a catchall tag for those on-top-of-the-stove pans that are spacious enough or designed specifically for fish. *Pierre Franey's Kitchen* recommends an oval-shaped, black steel pan that browns food and distributes heat well. The pan does need to be seasoned, but like a copper pot used only for beating egg whites, this one should be reserved for pan-frying fish only; with consistent use the pan should not be a bother to clean and maintain.

An oval flambé pan is a luxury to own, but, if you enjoy the results, this pan is a joy to have around. Its shape, an elongated oval, is perfect for fish. Try a stainless-steel-lined copper pan for efficiency.

John Dominis/Wheeler Pictures

Baking Dishes

Although you can use almost any baking dish for fish, there are a few that are designed specifically for the purpose. Made of enameled iron, stainless steel, stoneware, or porcelain, these oval-shaped dishes are perfectly shaped for fish cookery. Ready to go from oven to table, most of them are pleasing to look at as well. Measurements vary, but most come in sizes ranging from 12 inches by 8 inches by 1½ inches to about 16 inches by 10 inches by 2½ inches.

Cooking Parchment

Another "must" for oven cooking is parchment paper. Produce spectacular results with very little effort at a small cost by cooking en papillote (see page 86). Most parchment papers come in rolls similar to plastic wrap or aluminum foil containers. A roll that is 15 inches wide should suit most kitchen needs.

Molds

Not limited to baking, molds can be used for cool summer mousses, too. The three shapes most suited to seashore cookery are the scallop shell, curved fish, and straight fish. A savarin mold, recommends Pierre Franey, is a good choice for molds that are to be cooked on top of the stove in a hot-water bath. Choose molds that are tin, stainless steel, or that are lined with either of these. The good-quality copper molds are a splurge, definitely not a necessity.

Grilling

A sophisticated outdoor grill like this one makes preparing fish by the seashore easy—you don't have to spend time running in and out of the house for last-minute food preparation. If you're cooking over hot coals, it will make things easier if you use a fish grill. For best results, use fish steaks (be sure to trim them of their fat), whole dressed fish, or fillets with the skin still intact. Brush the grate with vegetable oil and turn the fish over once during the grilling time, following the Canadian rule (see page 79) for doneness. Watch the fish carefully to be sure it isn't cooking too quickly. Try adding dried fennel stalks or other dried herbs to the grill for a special treat.

SPECIALTY COOKWARE

Paella Pans

Chuck Williams of Williams-Sonoma is responsible for promoting the paella to popularity. As this book goes to press Mr. Williams is offering the public a choice of two, both with a 3-quart capacity: the original *cazuela*, the traditional earthenware pan that is fully glazed inside, with a partial glaze on the outside, and the more modern paella pan made of blue speckled enameled steel. You can also find aluminum and steel paella pans that will brown the ingredients well. The flat surface of the pans allows the short-grain rice to cook evenly; the sloping sides make it easier to serve portions that include a little of everything (you can rummage around for the morsels discreetly).

Woks

Many cooks choose not to bother with woks, but these Chinese-inspired pans are great if you like to stir-fry. Shaped like an upside down coolie hat in metal, a wok distributes heat evenly and keeps some ingredients warm on the upper edges of the pan, while you stir-fry others in the bottom. The cooking is quick and easy and relatively fat free because little oil is used and the food is fried *very* quickly. It is especially good for shellfish dishes.

If you're investing in a wok, choose one of rolled steel or iron rather than aluminum or thin stainless steel. You'll have to season the pan, but the extra time is well worth the trouble. Also consider buying a set of wok utensils: a flattish, wide spatula; a dipping basket; a shallow ladle; and a colander or steamer.

FANCIFUL FRILLS

Once you've bought all the cookware necessary for your kitchen, you should splurge on an unnecessary whimsical addition for your collection. Look around in antique shops for old copper molds or fish-shaped cookie cutters. Modern accoutrements include fish-shaped vol-au-vent cutters and skewers adorned with piscine and other animal likenesses.

Courtesy of Gardener's Eden

CHAPTER THREE

COOKING METHODS AND RECIPES

COOKING METHODS AND RECIPES

There's an elegance to cooking fish that lies in the simplicity of the preparation methods and the versatility of the sauces. Making a fish dinner can be a quick and easy choice or one involving hours of planning, shopping, and cooking. For instance, if you choose to broil fillets just under an inch thick, the cooking and preparation time should run no longer than ten minutes. With a delicate lemon-butter sauce or even a hollandaise, the prep time remains the same, because you can whip up the sauce while the fish is under the flame. The flip side, however, is that fish in all its deliciousness has the ability to reflect other tastes too. For stews and recipes calling for court-bouillon (see page 92), cooking can take as much as an hour or two.

Randy O'Rourke

Certain guidelines help when you're trying to decide how you want to cook a fish. Of course, budget and time restraints enter into the decision, but, overall, consider the following generalizations until you've gained a little experience.

- Oily, fattier fish tend to have a stronger, more distinctive flavor and, thus, should be cooked with less fat. Steaming, poaching, baking, broiling, and grilling are excellent choices.

- Leaner fish, with more delicate flavors, need more moisture in the cooking process. Baking, steaming, and poaching are good choices here, but pan-frying, deep-fat frying, stir-frying, and oven-frying are equally good alternatives.

- Dark meat generally indicates a higher fat content. White flesh is usually lean.

- Overcooking and cooking at too high a temperature are the two most frequent problems in cooking fish. When the thickest part of the flesh loses its transparency and flakes easily, the fish is done. (Following the instructions in a recipe gives you a formula that you should definitely observe, but thickness and size of the species vary to such a degree that some kitchen sense has to enter into the decision on when to remove the fish from the heat.)

- The Canadian Department of Fisheries has become well known for their "Canadian Rule," which recommends 10 minutes of cooking time for each 1 inch of fish thickness. Double the time for frozen fish. This rule applies to all fish cooking methods except stews, soups, and the like.

BAKING

One of the easiest methods of cooking fish, baking is best for whole, pan-dressed, and stuffed fish as well as fillets and steaks. Most recipes call for a preheated 350-degree oven. Rinse the fish quickly and pat it dry before placing it in a greased baking dish (or one that is lined with oiled baking paper). Arranging the fish in a single layer will facilitate cooking and serving. Follow the Canadian Rule for cooking time. Brush lean fish with melted butter or oil, and be sure that you baste if it's not prepared with liquids or a moist stuffing; seasoned broth, white wine, or a lemon-and-butter mixture work well. Baste, but do not use butter or oil with fatty fish, which should be cooked on a rack to allow the oils to drip into a shallow pan below. Some sources suggest scoring the skin to release the oils.

If you're baking a whole fish, test for flakiness where the flesh is thickest, down to the backbone, but also check to see if the fish has lost its translucency. With pan-dressed fish, put a pat of butter or rub some oil in the stomach cavity. Large fish can be wrapped in heavy-duty aluminum foil and placed on a baking sheet if they don't fit into a pan. Cooking en papillote is a quick, easy alternative that requires little fuss with beautiful results; for instructions, refer to page 86.

Gordon E. Smith, Courtesy *Family Circle*

Baking is a good method to use for roll-ups (left), the pan's sides hold the shapes firmly, and the fish benefits from the flavorful filling.

A whole, baked fish (right) can dress an informal table as a centerpiece, especially when it's garnished—in this case with fresh, perfect spinach leaves and scored lemon slices.

FLAMED SEA BASS

2 pounds sea bass fillets
$^2/_3$ cup butter, melted
1 teaspoon paprika
1 bunch kale
2 dozen parsley sprigs
2 tablespoons fennel seeds
$^1/_2$ cup brandy

Preheat the oven to 350 degrees. Divide the fish into serving portions. Place skin side down in a buttered or greased baking dish. Combine the butter and paprika and brush the mixture over the fish. Reserve the remaining sauce. Bake the fish using the Canadian Rule, or until the fish flakes easily when tested with a fork.

Rinse the kale and arrange it on the outer edge of a platter. Place the rinsed and dried parsley along the inner edge of the kale. Sprinkle the fennel seeds over the parsley. Place the fish in the middle of the platter so it is ringed by the greens. Pour the reserved butter sauce on the fish. Heat the brandy and flame it; then pour flaming brandy over the fish. **Serves 6.**

PLANKED SHAD

Planking has changed very little since Colonial times when the Indians and the settlers used planks over an open fire. The plank allows for cooking a butterflied fish on a broad surface, a tradition that the Dutch perfected. A butterflied fish, with its skin intact, is pinned—skin side down—onto a wood plank, preferably oak. Make sure that the wood has been cleaned and well oiled. Commercially sold wooden planks are available for use in the oven.

When cooking outside, use tacks or nails to secure the fish. How you prop the plank up is a matter of personal preference. One friend improvised a lean-to of sorts by hammering two sturdy branches into the ground. You'll have to estimate the distance from the flame to the plank. Time according to the Canadian Rule, but watch the fish carefully. If it seems to be cooking quickly, use the flake test for doneness.

Planking in the oven is an easier endeavor. Instructions follow.

3 pounds pan-dressed shad
2 tablespoons melted butter or oil
2 tablespoons fresh lemon juice
Salt to taste
Freshly ground black pepper to taste

Preheat the oven to 350 degrees and warm the plank. Combine all the ingredients, except the fish, and mix well. Place the fish on the heated plank and brush with the butter or oil mixture. Bake for 25 to 30 minutes, or until the fish flakes easily when tested with a fork. Serve with hot mashed potatoes, forming a ring around the fish, and garnish with parsley or hot cooked vegetables. Alternatively, serve with the shad roe soufflé. **Serves 6.**

Variations on a Theme

Two simple ways to bake a fish are variations on one basic theme.

For the first, choose a small pan-dressed fish. Roughly chop a small onion and a stalk of celery and combine; then add a pressed garlic clove and a leaf or two of fresh sage to the vegetables. Season with salt and freshly ground black pepper to taste. Stuff the mixture into the stomach cavity, adding a few pats of butter. Bake, basting with dry white wine or seasoned broth (the liquid should be 1/4 inch deep in the pan).

The second variation is to pat a mild-flavored, thin fish fillet dry and rub a half lemon over the flesh. Brush on melted butter. Prepare a stuffing using béchamel sauce, lemon juice, chopped and sautéed mushrooms, apples, chives, fresh parsley, and fresh tarragon. Season with more chives and a dollop of sour cream once the fish is on the plate. The ingredient amounts will vary according to the size of the fish and your own taste buds, but use your kitchen sense. A half cup of the mixture can easily stuff two fillets. Put the stuffing at the wider end of the fillet and roll it up. Place the fish seam side down in the pan. Baste with butter and a little dry white wine.

Gordon E. Smith

SHAD ROE SOUFFLÉ

Shad roe come in "sets," two pouches connected by a membrane that should not be severed before cooking. This American delicacy is often overlooked by seafood lovers. This recipe, although not a true soufflé in a proper soufflé dish, is a good accompaniment to planked shad.

1 pair shad roe
1 quart water
2 teaspoons, plus 1 tablespoon fresh lemon juice
1/4 cup butter
1/4 cup minced onion
1/2 cup all-purpose flour
1/2 teaspoon salt
1 cup milk
1/4 cup dry white wine
3 egg yolks, beaten
1/2 cup chopped fresh parsley
3 egg whites, beaten until stiff but not dry

Rinse the shad roe well and clean off any blood and veins. Make sure you don't break the membrane. Again, without tearing the membrane, prick it in a few places; this will prevent it from bursting. Soak in icy salted water for 5 minutes.

Combine the 1 quart of water and 2 teaspoons of lemon juice. Fill a large pot with just enough of the water and lemon juice solution to cover the shad, but bring the water to a simmer before adding the roe. Simmer for 3 to 10 minutes following the Canadian Rule (see page 79). Set aside and cool to room temperature.

In a saucepan, melt the butter. Add the onion and cook until tender. Blend in flour and salt. Gradually stir in the milk, wine, and remaining tablespoon of lemon juice. Heat the mixture until it thickens, stirring constantly. Stir in the parsley. Then fold in the egg whites and shad roe (membrane removed).

Cover the cooked planked shad with the soufflé. Return to the oven and bake for 10 to 15 minutes, or until the soufflé is done and brown. **Serves 6.**

Manuel Dos Passos

CAPE COD TURKEY WITH EGG SAUCE

Based on a recipe from Cape Cod, this gobbler was originally made with salt cod. Traditional accompaniments include boiled potatoes, beets, and onions. Don't choose this for your entrée if you want a dish that has modern verve. This one is steeped in American history.

2 pounds cod fillets
Salt
Freshly ground black pepper
4 tablespoons butter, melted
4 cups fresh bread crumbs
2 tablespoons diced onion
2 teaspoons chopped fresh dill
2 teaspoons chopped fresh parsley
1 teaspoon leaf thyme
2 eggs, beaten
Egg Sauce (recipe follows)
3 hard-boiled eggs, sliced (optional garnish)

Preheat the oven to 350 degrees. Sprinkle the fish with 1 teaspoon of salt and $1/2$ teaspoon of pepper. Place half the fillets in a well-greased (12- by 8- by 2-inch) baking dish.

In a bowl, combine the bread crumbs, 2 tablespoons of the melted butter, onion, dill, parsley, thyme, $1/2$ teaspoon of salt, a pinch of pepper, and the beaten eggs. Mix well and spread on top of the fillets in the baking dish. Place the remaining fillets on top of the stuffing mixture. Brush with the remaining 2 tablespoons of melted butter. Bake for 35 to 40 minutes, or until the fish flakes easily when tested with a fork. Serve with the Egg Sauce. Garnish by placing evenly sliced pieces of hard-boiled egg in a row along the length of the fish, one slightly on top of the next. **Serves 6.**

EGG SAUCE

$1/4$ cup butter
$1/3$ cup all-purpose flour
1 teaspoon dry mustard
1 teaspoon salt
$1/8$ teaspoon freshly ground white pepper
4 cups heavy cream or half-and-half
$1/2$ teaspoon hot pepper sauce
5 hard-boiled eggs, chopped
2 tablespoons chopped fresh parsley

In a saucepan, melt the butter. Stir in the flour, mustard, salt, and pepper. Add the cream gradually and cook over low heat until the sauce is thick and smooth, stirring constantly. Stir in the hot pepper sauce, eggs, and parsley.

SOLE MARGUERY

2 pounds sole fillets
Pinch of salt
Pinch of freshly ground black pepper
18 shucked raw oysters
18 shelled and deveined shrimp
Marguery Sauce (recipe follows)
1 cup fish fumet (see page 93), preferably made with sole trimmings

Preheat the oven to 350 degrees. Cut the fillets into serving-size portions. Sprinkle with salt and pepper. Place the oysters and shrimp in a well-greased 12- by 8- by 2-inch baking dish. Pour the fumet over the oysters and shrimp. Bake for about 15 minutes, or until the shrimp are pink. Remove the oysters and shrimp with a slotted spoon; set aside, and keep warm. Place the fillets in the baking dish with the fumet and bake according to the Canadian Rule, or until the fish flakes easily when tested with a fork. Remove the fish carefully to a broiling tray or ovenproof platter. Arrange 3 poached oysters and 3 poached shrimp on top of each serving. Cover with Marguery Sauce. Broil about 4 inches from the heat source until delicately browned, about 3 or 4 minutes. **Serves 6.**

MARGUERY SAUCE

1 cup fumet (see page 93), plus the pan juices from baking
1 cup butter
8 egg yolks, beaten
2 tablespoons fresh lemon juice
$^1/_4$ cup dry white wine

Combine the fumet and pan juices. Strain through a chinois or cheesecloth into a saucepan. Simmer very gently until reduced to $^1/_2$ cup. Add the butter and heat until melted. Beat in the egg yolks with a wire whisk. Continue beating over very low heat until the sauce thickens. Stir in the lemon juice and mix well. Add the wine and heat until hot enough to serve. Make sure you keep the heat low. **Makes about 2 cups of sauce.**

Simple garnishes—lemon slices, parsley, crab claws—transform an informal buffet into a party table. The star and tablecloths set the scene for the Fourth of July and coordinate the varied red, white, and blue dishware.

Recipe Robbery?

The recipe for fillets of sole Marguery was a secret formula known for many years by only a chosen few, including Monsieur Marguery, proprietor of the famed Restaurant Marguery in Paris, and Monsieur Mangin, the head chef. The code was broken with the help of Diamond Jim Brady, a turn-of-the-century bon vivant noted for his wealth and appetite. Brady had dined at Restaurant Marguery and enjoyed the fillets of sole Marguery so much that he tried to find the same dish at his favorite New York City restaurants after returning from Europe. When informed the recipe was known only to the chef and owner of the Restaurant Marguery, Brady persuaded one of his Manhattan restaurateur friends to send a member of his staff to Paris to learn the recipe. Rather than offend his best customer, it is reported, the New York restaurateur paid for his son to drop out of college and travel to France. After a year of kitchen espionage, the son returned to New York with the secret recipe. Brady, flaunting one of his many diamond stickpins, is said to have shown his appreciation by consuming nine orders of fillets of sole Marguery in a single meal.
—Ken Anderson
The Gourmet's Guide to Fish and Shellfish

Quick and Easy en Papillote

Parchment paper is not just a tool for bakers. By cutting a valentine out of the paper twice as large as a single serving of fish, you are well on your way to producing a striking, simple main course. Pop the fish on the paper, roll the edges to form an enclosed package, and voilà—individual packets of steaming hot, fragrantly spiced fish.

Once you've cut the parchment paper (or aluminum foil), unfold the heart shape and brush the inner surfaces with butter (or oil). Place the fish almost in the center, a little closer to the fold line than to the edges. Organize the rest of the ingredients as you wish, fold the paper over, and enclose by folding the edges over into a seam. Heat in a 400-degree oven for 8 to 10 minutes on a baking sheet. Remove from the oven and place one packet each on a plate. Guests should slit the parchment carefully because hot steam will escape.

A quick recipe uses just butter, lemon juice, and whatever fresh herb is around; sage or tarragon are my favorites. After brushing the butter on the parchment, rub the fish with a halved lemon and then brush it with more butter. Arrange the sage on top with a slice of lemon (to be removed by the guests), close up, and voilà.

Classic swordfish with rice makes an elegant serving when placed on metal dishes that reflect the table's candlelight.

SWORDFISH WITH CHUTNEY

$^1/_2$ cup chopped parsley
1 green chili pepper, sliced
3 garlic cloves, minced
4 tablespoons fresh lemon juice
$^1/_4$ cup water
$^1/_2$ teaspoon salt
1 teaspoon cumin seeds
$1^1/_2$ cups grated fresh coconut
1 to 2 teaspoons sugar
3 pounds swordfish fillets or steaks
$1^1/_2$ teaspoons freshly ground pepper
6 tablespoons butter
12 lemon wedges
Chopped parsley for garnish

Combine the parsley, green chili, garlic, lemon juice, and water in a blender until smooth and thick. Pour the mixture into a mixing bowl and add the salt, cumin, coconut, and sugar, stirring to combine the ingredients thoroughly into a chutney.

Cut the fish into 6 equal portions, each 1-inch thick. Season lightly with pepper. Place a teaspoon-size pat of butter on each of 6 pieces of aluminum foil (10 by 12 inches each) and cover it with a layer of the chutney, spreading the mixture so it will occupy about the same amount of space as a portion of the fish.

For each serving, place a piece of fish on top of the chutney. Distribute the rest of the chutney evenly over the top of each piece of fish. Dot each with an additional pat of butter. Fold over the edges of the aluminum foil so they form a loosely sealed package and place in the oven (on a baking sheet) or on a barbecue grill. Grill in oven at 425 degrees for about 10 minutes, then turn the packets and grill the other side for an additional 10 minutes. Serve with lemon wedges and sprinkle with chopped parsley. **Serves 6.**

Jeff McNamara (James Goslee III, stylist)

BROILING

Almost any fish takes to broiling, and the visual perfection of a well-broiled finny creature is hard to beat. You must, however, be careful not to let the flesh dry out. Since broiling exposes the fish to an open flame, the danger of ending up with tough or over-cooked meat is increased. Inch-thick pieces broil best at about 3 to 4 inches from the heat. I always line the bottom of the broiler pan with aluminum foil for easy cleanup. The removable, holed tray that fits into the pan should not be lined, because the holes must stay clear to allow the liquids to drain.

Preheat the broiler. The pan cooks the underside of the fish, which in most cases alleviates the need for turning a fillet over and possibly breaking it. Large fillets, steaks, and pan-dressed fish should, however, be turned about halfway through the cooking time. These larger or less-exposed pieces should be basted every few minutes. Many broiled fish are tastiest with just a lemon and butter sauce. Serve the fish immediately.

Broiling lends itself to somewhat sweet fruit sauces. The halibut, garnished with a dollop of sauce, is further enhanced by sprigs of fresh mint.

Salad and drinks at beachside prepare the palate for a broiled lunch either farther down the shore or at home. The complexity of the salad complements the simpler entrée.

John Dominis/Wheeler Pictures

BROILED SESAME MULLET

2 pounds mullet fillets
1/4 cup butter
2 tablespoons fresh lemon juice
2 tablespoons sesame seeds, toasted

Divide the fish into serving-size portions. Place the fish in a single layer, skin side down, on a well-greased baking pan. Heat the butter and add the lemon juice before the butter has completely melted. Baste the fish with the lemon-butter sauce. Then sprinkle with the sesame seeds.

Broil about 4 inches from the heat source following the Canadian Rule, or until the fish flakes easily when tested with a fork. Baste with any remaining sauce during the broiling time. The fish need not be turned. **Serves 6.**

Variation: Use benne seeds, a spicier relative of the sesame seed, which came to this country by way of the African slave trade in the 1600s. A handful of the seeds were believed to bring good luck and good health.

HERB BUTTER

Vary this recipe by using whatever fresh herbs you have access to: basil, parsley, cilantro, etc. Use the larger amount of the herb for a more powerful butter.

1/4 cup clarified butter
3 tablespoons fresh lemon juice
Pinch salt to taste
1 1/2 to 2 teaspoons fresh tarragon
1 teaspoon grated lemon zest

Brush the fish with the butter and broil as per the Broiled Sesame Mullet instructions. Garnish with scallions or parsley.

POACHING AND STEAMING

These related methods of cooking are favorites with diet-conscious fish lovers. The wet-cooking procedure insures a moist, flavorful fish with very little fat. Fish cooked this way are also good flaked in cold salads.

STEAMING

The easiest way to steam a fish is with a steamer made expressly for that purpose (see page 72), but an improvised rack or colander in a deep pan will work if you haven't invested in culinary equipment yet. Fill the pan with water just to the level of the rack; do not let the water touch the fish. Rinse and pat the fish dry.

If the fish has been skinned, you can either wrap it in cheesecloth with the material hanging out on two sides to form two "handles" for lifting, or you can use a commercially available vegetable spray or oil to make removal easier. Cheesecloth can help in getting the fish into and out of the pan even if you have a commercial steamer. Place the cloth under the steamer tray and gather it up and around, forming a tent-like covering. Let the cloth drop to the sides once the fish is in. A good pair of kitchen tongs can make lifting the cheesecloth out of the steamer easier.

Allow the water to come to a boil before you put the fish into the pan. Cover the steamer tightly. Many small fish and thin fillets may cook more quickly than the Canadian Rule allows for. Check for doneness using the flake test after 5 minutes, but don't check too often or the steam will lose its intensity.

POACHING

Poaching differs from steaming only in that you immerse the fish in the simmering liquid. A steamer or large skillet with a lid will do the trick for poaching. Use only enough liquid to just cover the fish; water, dry white wine, court-bouillon, and milk are the most common poaching bases. If you use milk, which is usually used for stronger-flavored fish, do not use lemon juice or vinegar because the combination will curdle.

The water should be just below a boil, to the point when the bubbles are barely visible.

Many poached fish recipes call for additions to the liquid. This is an area open for creativity and careful experimentation. Once you have the basics down pat, try combinations of spices, vegetables, poaching bases, and such to come up with your own recipe.

Use a white-wine based poaching liquid for salmon; strain, then add grated lime zest, lime juice, and white pepper to taste before reducing.

Steamed dishes work well in salads. A potpourri that includes a raw oyster, caviar, crab meat, and shrimp can be prepared quickly with a minimum of fuss. Take the time, however, to steam the necessary elements separately to preserve their unique tastes.

Reduction Action

Reducing the poaching liquid makes a good, simple sauce, but don't use heavily spiced or salty bases. Pour the liquid into a small saucepan and let it come to a boil (unless it's milk, which should come to a low simmer). Strain it into a clean skillet or small saucepan. In a bowl, mix a tablespoon of cornstarch with a little cold water and bring it to the consistency of sour cream. Stir constantly while you slowly add the cornstarch mixture to the poaching liquid. When it reaches the desired thickness, remove from the heat.

Judd Pilossof

COURT-BOUILLON

Court-bouillon is an overall name for a seasoned liquid such as a poaching liquid for fish. The most simple form is acidulated water (one quart water to every two or three tablespoons lemon and/or vinegar). You can also mix a half cup of red or white wine to a quart of water. And, of course, you can then add to the complexity by sprinkling in spices or slipping in some vegetables.

Manuel Dos Passos

MILD COURT-BOUILLON

2 quarts water
1 cup dry white wine
Juice of ¹/₄ lemon
1 large celery stalk with leaves
¹/₄ cup chunked carrot
2 Italian parsley sprigs
1 bay leaf
¹/₂ teaspoon salt
3 to 5 whole black peppercorns

Bring the liquids to a low boil. Cut the celery into chunks of at least 2 inches. Add the celery and the remaining ingredients to the boiling liquid. Fit a lid on loosely or make an aerated tent with aluminum foil. Simmer for 20 minutes; cool. You can strain this through a chinois or sieve, or you can use it to poach as it is.

FLAVORFUL COURT-BOUILLON

2 quarts water
1 cup dry red wine
¹/₈ cup balsamic or red wine vinegar
2 small onions, quartered
2 celery stalks with leaves, chunked
¹/₄ cup chopped fresh parsley or 4 chervil sprigs
2 bay leaves
2 whole cloves
2 thyme sprigs, or ¹/₂ teaspoon dried thyme
Freshly ground black pepper to taste

Follow the directions for mild court-bouillon, but simmer this broth for 45 minutes. Use for stronger-tasting fish.

PATRICK VERRÉ'S COURT-BOUILLON

This is a classic that can be used in almost any recipe calling for court-bouillon, including Café 43's recipe for sea bass wrapped in lettuce with lobster stuffing and truffle sauce (see page 45).

1 medium onion
4 celery ribs
1 carrot
1 tablespoon white vinegar
2 cups white wine
White pepper to taste
1 bay leaf
Pinch thyme
Pinch chervil
Pinch parsley
1¹/₂ quarts water

Sweat the vegetables (onion, carrot, celery), then add the vinegar, white wine, and white pepper to taste. Add the bay leaf, thyme, chervil, parsley, and water. Let simmer for 30 minutes.

FISH FUMET

Also known in simpler terms as fish stock, fumets are as varied as court-bouillons. They differ from court-bouillons in that they are simmered with the fish trimmings. Try to avoid using fatty fish such as mackerel or mullet, unless you're planning to poach salmon, in which case you should use salmon trimmings. Fumets are classically used for aspics, sauces, and soups.

1¹/₂ pounds lean fish bones and
   trimmings (heads, backbones,
   skin of whole, drawn fish, etc.)
2 tablespoons butter
1 onion, chopped
¹/₄ cup chopped carrots
3 mushrooms, quartered
2 celery stalks with leaves
3 to 4 parsley sprigs or chervil
1 bay leaf
2 small pieces lemon rind
Dash of lemon juice
1 cup dry white wine or Sauternes
1 cup water

Rinse the fish trimmings and cut them into big chunks. In a stockpot, melt the butter and sauté the onion, carrots, and mushrooms just until the onion is translucent but not browned. Cut the celery into large chunks and add it to the pot. Put the fish trimmings and the rest of the ingredients into the pot. Bring the mixture to a boil, skim, and simmer for 20 minutes. Strain the liquid from the mixture through a chinois, sieve, or muslin. To reduce further, pour the liquid into a clean saucepan and simmer over low heat. Let cool. Freeze or store in the refrigerator.

Variation: Add a bit of clam juice (bottled or fresh) 5 minutes before straining.

Sandra Dos Passos

ASPIC AT A GLANCE

Fish aspics are really nothing more than poached fish in a gelatin-based glaze. You begin with a degreased poaching stock, but since the aspic will be on show, it is necessary to clarify the liquid until it is perfectly clear.

Let the poaching stock cool. For every two cups of stock to be used, beat one egg white slightly. Keep the eggshells and crush them. Combine one package of unflavored gelatin with a small amount of the cooled fumet (see note below). Add the whites and shells to the stock and bring to a simmer. Make sure the stock does not boil; push the egg whites to the side of the pan gently if necessary. Simmer for 5 minutes and remove from the heat very carefully, so as not to disturb the whites. Allow the stock to rest for at least 10 minutes; the egg whites will cause impurities to rise to the surface. Moisten enough cheesecloth to line a colander with two layers. Put the colander over a large bowl. Skim the crust and ladle the liquid into the colander. The result should be the consistency of thick syrup.

If you're presenting a whole fish, use a platter that has a lip and ladle the aspic over the fish. Decorate (see box) and chill.

If you're using a mold and poached fish flakes, rinse the mold and coat first with the aspic and then with the fish; repeat. Make sure you end with aspic. Level with a knife as you would dry ingredients in a measuring cup. Tap the bottom of the mold gently to release any air bubbles. You can also decorate a mold by using a number of garnishes, following the designs of the molded impression. Ready your serving platter before you unmold by wiping it with a damp cloth. Insert a knife into the sides of the mold here and there; do not run the knife along the entire edge of the mold. Put the platter on top of the mold and turn the two over together. Cover with a dish towel moistened with hot water.

Note: Fumet has a tendency to thicken on its own a bit without gelatin. Ruth Spear, in her book *Cooking Fish and Shellfish*, recommends testing the stock. Place a small saucer in the freezer until it's cold. Remove it, spoon a tablespoon or so of the stock into the dish, and refrigerate for 10 minutes. If no jelling occurs, add the gelatin package. If it's only partially jelled; add half.

A basic rule of thumb for stews: sauté the vegetables before adding the cooking liquid. Simmer as necessary, being careful not to overcook the fish.

Garnish Fit for a Fish

The fun in making aspics is in the last step: decorating. Use your imagination and whatever suits your fancy to garnish the whole fish or the mold. Follow the theme of the mold or be wild and imitate modern art or your favorite geometric design. Create with subtlety, though; you want your guests to remember the taste more than the effect. Use the list below as a source for ideas.

Capers
Cucumbers—sliced thinly and soaked briefly in salted water
Eggs—hard-boiled and sliced thinly
Greens—chives, dill, parsley, scallions, watercress, even coriander in small doses
Lemons—sliced thinly or slivers of the rind
Olives—pitted and sliced
Reds—roasted peppers or pimientos
Truffles—sparingly

You can also use any of these as base materials to cut and use on the basis of their color. White from the eggs, yellow from the yolks and lemons. Greens. Reds. Black from truffles.

Using a toothpick or kitchen tweezers, pick each piece up and dip it into the aspic in the pan before placing on the fish or in the mold.

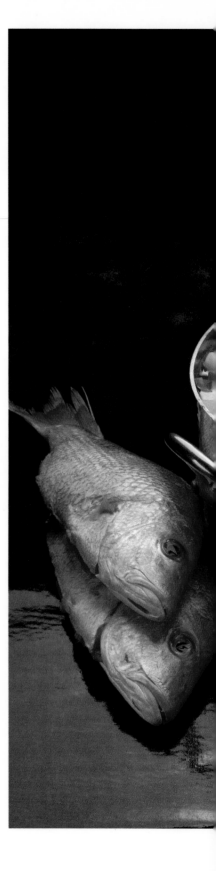

PORTUGUESE FISHERMAN STEW

This stew is a European–New England blend. The tomatoes, olive oil, and spices reflect its Portuguese origins; the pumpkin and corn add a touch of Americana.

2 pounds striped bass fillets
1 tablespoon sweet butter
1 tablespoon olive oil
1 cup chopped onion
3 garlic cloves, crushed
1/4 teaspoon crushed red pepper
1 green pepper, seeded and chopped
6 plum tomatoes, peeled and chopped
1 cup fish fumet (see page 93)
1/2 cup dry white wine
1 cup water
2 teaspoons chopped fresh basil
3 thyme sprigs
Salt and freshly ground black pepper to taste
2 to 3 cubed cups winter squash or pumpkin
2 ears sweet corn, cut into pieces

Rinse the fish and cut it into 1-inch cubes. Set it aside.

Melt the butter and oil in a large saucepan. Add the onion, garlic, and red pepper; cook until tender but not brown. Add the green pepper and tomatoes and combine with the onion mixture. Add fish fumet, wine, water, basil, thyme, and salt and pepper and bring to a low boil. Add the squash and corn. Cover and simmer for 10 to 15 minutes, or until the squash and corn are done. Add the fish and cook for 5 to 10 minutes, or until the fish flakes easily when tested with a fork. **Serves 6 to 8.**

You may have noticed *panfish* at your local fish shop. These finny delights are usually described as small whole fish just big enough to fit into a standard pan. Obviously there is a lot of interpretation in that statement. How big is the pan? How big is the fish? Your judgment should depend on what pans you have available in your kitchen and how big your appetite is. One fish to a person can make an elegant presentation at the dinner table. Alternatively, you can use coated fillets. As in deep-fat frying, if you pan-fry successfully, the juices of the fish will be sealed in, resulting in an arresting succulence.

Although the method is most commonly used for freshwater whole fish, it is well suited for cooking smelt and locally caught small species that may not be common commercially. To reiterate, this method is best for small fish, no more than 1 inch thick. The cooking time reflects this; each side takes from between 2 and 4 minutes to crisp.

If desired, you can remove the head and the tail. Wipe the fish, making sure that it is dry. That's where agreement among the experts ends. Some cooks recommend dipping the fish in milk or a beaten egg-and-water combination (1 egg to 2 tablespoons water); others forego this. The next step—seasoning and dusting—has even more variations (refer to "Coating Controversy," page 97) according to personal taste.

Pour $1/4$ inch to $1/2$ inch of fat into a large pan—preferably a combination of vegetable oil and butter. Don't use olive oil, but do use clarified butter if you can. The purer butter helps prevent the fat from burning (see box on page 98). Heat the fat until a drop of water will sizzle in it; if it smokes, the heat is too high. Keep the temperature as high as you can without letting the fat burn or smoke. The intensity of the heat is the key to pan-frying. Adjust as necessary throughout the process.

Place the fish or fillets in the pan in a single layer. Peek underneath just as you would to see if a pancake were properly browned. When the fish is golden, it's ready to flip. Use a spatula and turn carefully so as not to break the fillet. The frying time for the second side will be about 1 minute less than for the first side.

Again, keeping the temperature evenly hot is important, so as soon as one fillet is done, place another in the pan. If you absolutely must add more fat, heat it separately before adding it to the pan; avoid doing this if you can, though.

When the fish are ready, drain on absorbent paper towels. Serve immediately.

Fried shrimp need not have a heavy batter coating—especially when combined with crisp, fresh lettuce and green and red pepper for a delicious main course salad.

Courtesy of Crate and Barrel

James Goslee III

WALNUT FRIED FLOUNDER

2 pounds flounder fillets
$^{1}/_{2}$ teaspoon salt
$^{1}/_{4}$ teaspoon freshly ground black pepper
$1^{1}/_{2}$ cups plain cracker crumbs
$1^{1}/_{2}$ cups ground walnuts
$1^{1}/_{2}$ teaspoons crushed dried rosemary
1 teaspoon dried marjoram leaves
$^{1}/_{2}$ teaspoon leaf thyme
1 cup all-purpose flour
2 eggs, beaten
$^{1}/_{3}$ cup butter
$^{1}/_{3}$ cup cooking oil
Lemon wedges

Rinse the fish and pat it dry. Sprinkle with salt and pepper. Combine the cracker crumbs, walnuts, rosemary, marjoram, and thyme. Dust the fillets with the flour, dip in the eggs, and roll in the crumb mixture.

Heat the butter and oil in a skillet until hot but not smoking. Place the fish in the pan and fry following the Canadian Rule. The fish should be nicely browned. Turn carefully halfway through the cooking time. Drain on absorbent paper toweling. Serve with the lemon wedges. **Serves 6.**

Clarifying Butter

To inexperienced cooks, clarified butter may sound like liquid gold—hard to come by and expensive to produce—but it's actually quite simple and the results are more than satisfying. Each cup of butter reduces to about ³/₄ of a cup, so figure out how much you need for your recipe before you begin cooking.

Cut unsalted, sweet butter into pats and melt it over low heat. Put it aside until you can see the milk solids resting on the bottom and the butter fat on top. First skim the butter fat off the top; then pour the clear butter, avoiding the solids, into another container. Set aside until ready to use. You can also refrigerate clarified butter.

Jeff McNamara

SCANDINAVIAN SMELT FRY

20 medium-size smelt or other small fish
1 two-ounce can anchovy fillets
¹/₄ teaspoon freshly ground black pepper
¹/₂ cup all-purpose flour
3 tablespoons butter
3 tablespoons oil
4 slices rye bread, crusts removed, toasted
Scandinavian Sauce (recipe follows)
Lemon twists and dill sprigs for garnish

Remove the heads from the fish; then clean and bone the fish. Drain the anchovies, reserving the oil for the sauce. Cut the anchovies in half lengthwise. Place half an anchovy inside each fish. Sprinkle the fish with pepper; then roll in the flour.

In a large skillet, heat the butter and oil, but do not allow it to smoke. Add the fish and fry until crisp. Place 5 fish on each slice of rye toast. Spoon some sauce over the smelts and garnish with lemon twists and dill sprigs. Serve with sliced tomatoes and cucumbers. **Serves 4.**

SCANDINAVIAN SAUCE

Reserved anchovy oil from above
2 tablespoons minced onion
1 cup heavy cream or half-and-half
1 egg yolk, beaten
1 tablespoon fresh lemon juice
1 tablespoon minced fresh dill

In a saucepan, cook the onion in anchovy oil until tender. Blend in the cream gradually and cook until thickened, stirring constantly. Add a little of the heated sauce to the egg yolk; then add to the remaining sauce, stirring constantly. Heat until thickened. Add the lemon juice and dill. **Makes 1 cup of sauce.**

John Dominis/Wheeler Pictures

POMPANO MEUNIERE

2 pounds pompano fillets
1 cup flour
1 teaspoon salt
1/4 teaspoon cayenne pepper
3/4 cup butter clarified
Juice of half lemon
Chopped parsley

Rinse fish and remove any bones or skin in the fillets. Cut into 6 equal portions. Combine the flour, salt, and pepper on a clean, flat surface. Dip the fish portions into the seasoned flour, being sure to coat both sides of the fillets.

Heat 1/2 cup of the clarified butter in a skillet until the fish turns a light brown, turn, and drain on absorbent paper. Keep the first fish portions warm while sautéeing the last few pieces. Place each portion of fish on a heated plate readied for the table. Then, rinse the skillet, wipe dry, and heat the remaining clarified butter over high heat until it foams; add a squeeze or two of lemon juice. Pour directly on to each fish piece, sprinkle with parsley, and serve immediately. **Serves 6.**

Smelt and other small fish are often overlooked in American markets. Pan-fried until crisp, they make an excellent summer snack.

STIR-FRYING

Stir-frying has become a classic among today's harried cooks. It requires preparation time, to be sure, but once all the ingredients are laid out and ready, you can cook in a flash.

Borrowed and adapted from the Chinese, stir-frying can be used for both fat or lean fish. Rinse the fish and pat it dry. Cut into pieces about $1^1/_2$ inches long. Prepare a marinade of a little coarse salt (kosher salt as opposed to sea salt), the whites of 2 small eggs, 1 heaping tablespoon of cornstarch, and roughly about $^1/_4$ cup of vegetable oil (use pure soy or peanut oil if you can find it). Mix together well. Let the fish marinate in a covered container in the refrigerator for no more than $^1/_2$ hour.

Heat a wok (see page 75) or a big skillet and pour in a very light coating of oil. Spread the oil over the bottom and sides of the pan. When a drop of water sizzles in the oil, you're ready to add the fish and whatever else—cut vegetables, garlic, other spices—you want. Stir constantly keeping the fish moving but in contact with the pan. Use a slotted spoon or Chinese basket strainer to remove the fish to a serving dish. Serve immediately.

Sandra Dos Passos

Judd Pilossof

Prepare all the ingredients for a stir-fried dish beforehand. Set them aside in separate bowls according to their cooking time. The initial preparation eliminates interruptions and helps to ensure flash-fried food with a fresh flavor.

OVEN-FRYING

If you're watching your weight or your fat intake, but you can't do without fried foods, you may want to try this method of cooking fish. Technically, this is not frying but baking at a high temperature. You use less oil than deep-fat frying. In addition, the procedure is not as time consuming or messy. Steaks and fillets are most appropriate for oven frying.

Preheat the oven to 500 degrees. Have on hand a large baking pan in which you can put a single layer of fish without crowding. Lightly oil the pan before proceeding. Rinse the fish and pat dry. Dip each piece of fish first into milk or into an egg-and-milk combination (1 egg for every 2 tablespoons of milk). Then dip into a readied bowl of lightly toasted bread crumbs. Coat the fish on both sides. Take care when moving the fish from the crumb bowl to the baking pan. If the fish has its skin, place it skin side down. Melt ¹/₂ cup of butter (which should be sufficient for four servings) and pour equal amounts on each fish. You'll probably have to add a few minutes to the basic Canadian Rule because of the coating in this case. Baking time should be between 10 and 15 minutes. For a slight variation add ¹/₂ teaspoon of lemon juice to the butter and reduce the quantity of butter.

Oven-fried fish are beginning to reappear on sophisticated tables. Use an oven thermometer to make sure the temperature is *hot*. For a luncheon, set an Americana-inspired table.

It's easier to pull off the end of shrimp tails if they are kept free of coating. Serve the sauce on the side to keep the shrimp crisp. Remember, too, to drain the shellfish well before placing them on the platter.

DEEP-FAT FRYING

So many people inadvertently ruin fried fish that it's sometimes hard to defend this process. When done properly, however, deep-fat frying achieves crisp, juicy results. Granted, it's much maligned because when poorly prepared it is laden with calories and fat, but in any form to some it's a comfort food that brings back fond memories of childhood.

This type of frying works best with lean fillets. It is crucial that the fish be dry (after rinsing) for the batter to stick well. Equally important is the oil: Don't let it reach the smoking point and don't reuse oil in which the solids have not been strained out. With these two caveats in mind, you will most likely not have to deal with overpowering "fried" odors. The amount of oil you use depends on the cookware you have. For a deep-fat fryer or tall saucepan, use three inches of oil; a little less for electric frying pans, woks, and the like.

Heat the oil to 375 degrees. Use a thermometer!

Dip the fish pieces in beaten egg, milk, or flour and then in batter, cracker crumbs, cornmeal, or—if you haven't already used flour—flour. Don't overcrowd the fish either on your preparatory platter or in the frying pan. Better to make another batch than to crowd.

Submerge the fish in the hot oil and drain on absorbent paper toweling. Cook according to the Canadian Rule. If you're using a wok, turn the fish once.

Check the temperature of the oil between each batch. Don't disregard this warning. Frying at too low a temperature will soak the fish with grease; frying at too high a temperature will produce smells that I can assure you you won't want around. If you need to add fresh oil, do so in between each batch when you can regulate the temperature.

Gordon E. Smith, Courtesy *Family Circle*

BEER BATTER

Use this recipe for deep-fat frying fish or shellfish.

1 cup beer
1 cup flour
1/2 teaspoon baking powder
1 teaspoon salt
1/8 teaspoon freshly ground black pepper

Combine the ingredients in a mixing bowl and blend thoroughly, adding additional beer if necessary to produce a smooth, thick batter. Use immediately or refrigerate. **Makes about 1 cup.**

NOTES ON SHELLFISH

With a few exceptions, you can use the information for cooking fish and apply it to shellfish. The rules for broiling, baking, pan-frying, deep-fat frying, poaching, and steaming are similar. Cooking times vary, though, as does initial preparation. Below, and in the text in Chapter Two, you'll find instructions for readying and cooking the most common shellfish, mollusks, and bivalves in the United States.

Clams, ready for steaming in their shells; mussels, open and ready to eat; raw shrimp; and lobster are a great combination especially when garnished with lemon and washed down with a light white wine.

Crab, shrimp, and clams are delectable shellfish that will satisfy discriminating palates.

John William Lund

Abalone

Found most commonly along the California shore, abalone is now subject to strict rules for gathering; once ignored by fishermen, the univalve mollusk has entered into mainstream gourmet markets and its fresh meat is available commercially only in California. Outside of the Golden State, consumers can buy canned abalone, which may be used in any recipe calling for the fresh product.

Either fresh or canned, abalone must be prepared well for it to taste good; overcooking will cause the flesh to become rubbery and unappetizing. It's a mild-flavored mollusk, so plan to serve a spicy accompaniment, such as an oyster sauce or a ginger and garlic sauce.

If you're buying the abalone fresh, shuck by forcing a wedge between the meat and the shell. Separate the flesh from the viscera and fringe portions. Wash and slice across the grain. Pound thin slices with a mallet to tenderize them. You can pan-fry these slices in a flash (45 to 50 seconds per side) or use them in chowder (blanch or poach them before chopping or mincing).

Anyone who has seen shell middens, piles of broken shells left by prehistoric man, can attest to the long-standing habit of eating clams. Yet, confusion still reigns over which clams are which. The West Coast commercial species are fairly easily recognized: geoducks, razors, and gapers. It's on the East Coast where the problem begins. The cherrystone, littleneck, and quahog are all the same clam at different stages or sizes in the lifecycle. This hard-shell clam, commonly pronounced co-hog, is referred to as the littleneck when it's at its smallest edible size; when it's a bit larger—ranging up to about 3 inches in diameter—it is known as a cherrystone. Beyond that it's a chowder clam because the meat is no longer as tender as at the littler stages. The other common name, the steamer, refers to the soft-shell clam or longneck clam. Last, there is the surf or sea clam, which is most often canned or used in chowders.

CLEANING

Once you've scrubbed the outsides, many clams will clean themselves internally with a little initial human intervention. Place the clams in a bucket or large soup pot with fresh sea water or cold salted water (1 cup of salt to each gallon of fresh water or 1 teaspoon of salt to a quart). Use the saltwater solution if you think the sea water you have access to may be polluted. Do not put the clams in fresh water! Add a cup or a few handfuls of cornmeal to the bucket. Soak the clams for 6 hours. Keep them cool and out of direct sunlight. Change the water a few times and rinse the bucket

Stuff shells with clams and breadcrumbs, a mushroom-béchamel, or a spinach-and-parmesan combination. For a trendier taste, invent a stuffing with nuts, sun-dried tomatoes, or citrus sauce.

to remove the sand and grit that will accumulate. Discard any open clams.

TO OPEN A CLAM

It's simple but not that simple. Old hands offer different instructions for each type of clam, and, as in most "traditional" cooking arts, there are variations based on temperament and training. All sources seem to agree, however, that clams should be chilled before opening. Either put them in the freezer for an hour or so or submerge them in water and ice cubes. Do all your opening over a bowl so you can catch the clam liquor. Once you're done, you can strain the liquid through a double layer of cheesecloth.

Cherrystone clams: A large, blunt clam knife works best here because the shells are hard and heavy. Cup the clam in one hand with the flat side down. Put the knife edge by the groove at the hinge. Curl your middle three or last four fingers up and just a bit over the blade. Put pressure on the knife and try to slip the blade in without moving it back and forth, an action that might break the shell. Get the knife in just a bit and twist with one quick motion. Once the shell is open, you can run the knife around the inside and end by severing the muscle by the upper shell. Be careful not to mar the meat.

Littleneck clams: Use a narrow-bladed, somewhat pointy clam knife, for these shells are more fragile. Follow the instructions above.

Geoducks: This large clam has been known to grow to 8 pounds, a rare weight for a rare clam. Don't try to shuck these giants; rather, place them in boiling wa-

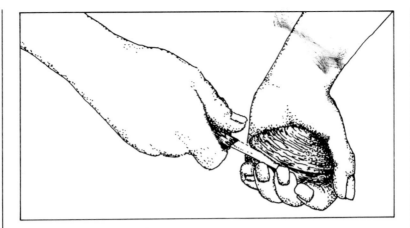

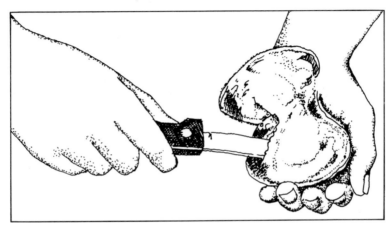

ter and wait for the shells to open. Use a small fillet knife to sever the muscle.

Razor and gaper clams: You'll want to use a small fillet knife to shuck these clams because of their size, too. Make sure the shell hinge is nestled in the palm of your hand. The shell opening should be toward you. Insert the knife blade into the groove at the rear of the clam to sever the muscle. Try to get the blade between the meat and shell so you cut only the muscle. Then run the knife along the shell and cut the other muscle near the neck. Work from foot to neck. Trim so you save the meat only.

For razor clams, you'll have to trim the neck with scissors or a small fillet knife. Split lengthwise or leave whole. With gapers, trim the neck closer to the body of the clam. If you're having trouble peeling the skin from the neck, blanch in boiling water for 25 seconds. For all of them, make sure you trim off the dark parts and the viscera and discard them. You can eat the neck and the cleaned "belly."

AN ALTERNATIVE

If you'll be cooking the clams, you can facilitate shucking them by first steaming them for a minute or by pouring boiling water on them. If you opt for the latter, allow the clams to sit for 1 minute; then transfer them quickly to a pot of cold water. One last alternative is to place the clams in a 450-degree oven for several minutes—not to exceed 5 minutes. Make sure they are arranged in a single layer, and discard any that are not open.

THE ROGUE'S RED CLAM CHOWDER

Although a red chowder is usually associated with Manhattan, The Rogue restaurant in Monterey, California, has come up with a winning combination that rivals any from the Big Apple. This is a good addition to a clambake or autumn barbecue.

1 pound clarified butter (see page 98)
1 cup diced onion
1 green pepper, diced
1/4 cup diced bacon
1 ounce salt pork, diced
1 cup diced celery
1 cup all-purpose flour
1 can tomato puree and 1 can crushed tomatoes, or 4 cups fresh tomatoes
2 cups water
2 quarts clam juice, preferably fresh
2 tablespoons crushed garlic
1 tablespoon sweet basil
1 teaspoon thyme
Salt and freshly ground black pepper to taste
2 pounds potatoes, diced
2 1/2 pounds clams, chopped

Heat the clarified butter in a large skillet. Add the onion, pepper, bacon, pork, and celery and sauté until all are soft. Add the flour and cook for 10 minutes, stirring occasionally. Add the tomatoes, water, clam juice, and seasonings. Simmer for 1 hour. Add the potatoes and clams and simmer until the potatoes are tender. **Serves 10 to 12.**

Note: If the chowder is too thick, add more clam juice.

COOKING CLAMS

Many of the methods for cooking fish can be used or adapted for clams. Certainly deep-fat frying and pan-frying are common methods used along the shores in clam shacks and even in some elegant resort dining rooms. Shake the clams in a paper bag filled with a bit of flour; then dip in a beaten egg and then in cracker crumbs or a coating of your choice. Fry in hot oil for about 5 minutes, or until golden brown. One local recipe from Maine that was sent to me by a friend suggests making a batter by mixing an egg yolk with a pat or two of butter which has been melted; then adding 1/2 cup of milk and 1/2 cup or so of flour; add the flour slowly, mixing after each addition.

Steamed clams are a delicacy, especially when you use a dry white wine instead of water; the smaller the clams, the better. Timing is easy: you steam the clams—on a rack—until the shells open, usually 4 or 5 min-utes. Discard any that haven't opened and strain the liquid through cheesecloth to use for dipping. (Euell Gibbons in his wonderfully informative and somewhat outdated book—*Stalking the Blue-Eyed Scallop*—which is now, unfortunately, out of print, warns not to steam razor clams. I've never had them steamed, but I'd heed the wise man's caveat.)

I'm admitting to simple tastes here, but one of my most distinct childhood memories is of the too-hot-to-touch golden brown clam cakes in the Rhode Island building at the Eastern States Exposition in West Springfield, Massachusetts. The recipe came from the side of the Kenyon's Johnny Cake Cornmeal package (see Appendix Two). Whether it was the setting, the novelty of the fair, or the actual clams, I'll never know, but to me these clam fritters are just the right addition to a family gathering or even an informal supper among friends.

Blue Beach (color woodcut on paper, 12½″ x 13⅞″) by Mary Mullineux.

CLAM PIE

3 dozen shell clams or 24 ounces canned
1½ cups water
4 to 6 mushrooms, sliced
1 small onion, chopped
¼ cup butter
¼ cup all-purpose flour
¼ teaspoon dry mustard
⅛ teaspoon hot pepper sauce
¼ teaspoon salt
⅛ teaspoon white pepper
1 cup reserved clam liquor
1 cup cream or half-and-half
1 tablespoon lemon juice
2 tablespoons parsley, chopped
2 tablespoons pimiento, chopped (optional)
Pastry for a 1-crust 9-inch pie
1 egg

Wash clam shells thoroughly. Place clams in a large pot of water; bring to a boil and then simmer for 8 to 10 minutes or until clams open. Remove the clams from the shells and cut into fourths. Reserve 1 cup of clam liquor. (If using canned clams, drain and reserve 1 cup of the liquor. Cut the clams in half.)

Slice the mushrooms and chop the onion. Set aside. Melt the butter in a skillet. Add the mushrooms and the onion and cook until tender but not brown. Stir in the flour, mustard, hot pepper sauce, salt, and pepper. Gradually add the clam liquor and the cream or half-and-half. Cook, stirring constantly, until thick. Stir in lemon juice, parsley, pimiento (if desired), and clams.

Pour mixture into a 9-inch round deep-dish pie plate (about 2 inches deep). Roll out the pastry dough and place on top of the mixture in the pie plate; secure the dough to the rim of the pie plate by crimping. Vent pastry. Brush with beaten egg. Bake in a 375 degree oven for 25 to 30 minutes or until pastry is browned. **Makes 6 servings.**

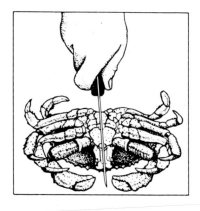
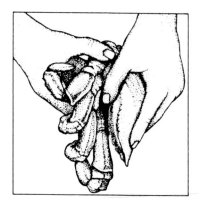
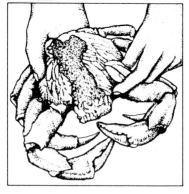

Kurt J. Wallace (from *The Gourmet's Guide to Fish and Shellfish*)

1. Place the crab upside down on a cutting board. Position the knife and quickly and forcefully bring it down along the crab's center. Or hit the positioned knife with a mallet. Either method kills the crab instantly. 2. Now pry open the top shell in one easy motion using your hands. 3. Remove the viscera, gills, and spongy parts; rinse the crab thoroughly under cool running water. Split the body in half and then into pieces to facilitate getting at the small pieces of meat. 4. Pry off the claws and each leg; use a mallet to crack them.

King crab mixes well with a homemade scallion mayonnaise. The avocado halves, rubbed first with lemon juice, are perfect serving dishes for a casual lunch.

Crabs

Although most diners won't come across the Tasmanian giant crab, which has been known to weigh as much as thirty pounds, all crabs *are* edible. In fact, the practice of eating crabs dates back to circa 20,000 B.C. In the United States the more well-known possibilities include the tiny pea crab found living in oyster shells, with the oysters; rock and Jonah crabs of New England; blue and stone crabs from more southerly shores; and the Alaskan king crab and the Dungeness, which are found on the West Coast.

Gordon E. Smith

HARD-SHELL BLUE CRABS

As with many processes involving seafood preparation, there is more than one way to clean and cook a blue crab. The controversy in this case is one of timing: Do you cook the crab before cleaning it or after? There are three main advantages to cleaning before cooking. First, since most of any given hard-shell crab is waste, if you clean the crab prior to cooking you will be putting more edible crab meat in the pot. Second, you will be able to cool the crab meat more quickly, making it easier to shell. Last, if you remove the viscera before you cook, you lose the gamey taste that the entrails give to the crab meat when the crab is cooked intact. Some crab devotees will argue about this last point; they like the crab taste in all its fullness. My recommendation is to try both methods and decide for yourself.

To cook the crab first, you simply plunge the washed crab into a pot of boiling salted water (approximately 1 tablespoon salt for each quart of water); cook for 20 to 25 minutes. Crack the carapace and pull the top of the shell off, or, if you can, open the tail flap and pull it against the carapace; doing the latter should remove the top shell. Scrape out the gills, spongy substances, and all of the inner skeleton to reveal the sweetest meat of the backfin. Use a crab knife, nutpick, and nutcracker to capture as much of the meat as you can.

Cleaning the live crab before you cook it is a trickier endeavor. The first few times that you try this you will undoubtedly be pinched. Rubber gloves seem to help, but practice more than anything else is the cure-all for crab "bites." The best directions I've come across are in a gem of a book called *Keeping the Catch* by Kenn and Pat Oberrecht. Come in from behind the crab and grab the right claw and right legs in your right hand. Do the same on the left side with your left hand. Try to get close in to the crab's body, as this helps to keep the crustacean from moving too much. Grasp with as tight a grip as you can, because the next step is the most difficult. You want to line up the edge of the crab's carapace with the edge of a steady table or counter. Push downward. The carapace will come away from the crab. Don't loosen your grip. Now you must break the crab in half "by first bending the legs downward, then upward again, until the two halves come apart—as if you were breaking a 'green' stick or tree branch," write the Oberrechts. Shaking the crab over a proper receptacle will remove most of the viscera. Scrape out the rest and the gill and spongy parts; then rinse under cold water. (I admit I'm somewhat squeamish and choose to cook the crabs first, and that is a factor to take into consideration.)

Cooking the precleaned crabs is similar to the cooking instructions for the whole crabs. Prepare a pot of salted boiling water, making sure there is enough water to cover all the crabs. Cook for about 20 to 25 minutes.

If you plan to save the shells for serving and have cleaned the crabs before cooking, plunge the shells into boiling water. Rinse them in cold water and dry.

SOFT-SHELL BLUE CRABS

These tasty crabs are not a distinct species set apart from their hard-shell brothers; they are only in a different stage of life. Crabs molt every so often as they grow, shedding their hard shells for a newer, larger shell. The carapace is soft just after molting and is supple only for a few days. In this state, the crabs—especially blue crabs—are famous.

To clean soft-shell crabs, turn them with their face downward on a cutting board. Insert a sharp, pointed knife just behind the crab's "eyes" and cut out the "face." Peel the flap of the shell back and remove the sandbag and spongy material. Scrape out the viscera and wash under cool running water.

Sauté them in butter, broil them for about 10 minutes with a pat of butter and a squeeze of lemon juice, or deep-fat fry them with a dried bread crumb coating. The last takes only 3 to 5 minutes.

OYSTER CRABS

For a real treat, sauté up some oyster crabs. These tiny creatures reside inside oyster shells. They don't harm the oyster, nor do they help it; they just live there. Many folks discard the crabs thinking they are not edible. But try them. When they turn golden brown in the pan, they're ready. Turn them onto toast and serve them with a side of tartar sauce.

Jeff McNamara (James Goslee III, stylist)

DUNGENESS CRABS

The sweet meat of a Dungeness crab has become legendary. James Beard in his autobiographical book *Delights & Prejudices* says of them: "If you allow these [fresh Dungeness crabs] to cool and eat them with a rich homemade mayonnaise, good bread and butter, and beer or a very light wine, you will have a meal that the gods intended only for the pure in palate." To follow this great chef's lead, you must take yourself down to the wharves in San Francisco or the cities of the coastal Northwest. Refrigerated Dungeness crabs that have been shipped across the country are only second best. But they still are tasty!

If you're cleaning the crab before cooking it, follow the illustrated instructions (see page 110) unless you want to present the crab as a whole at the table. In that case, follow the instructions up to rinsing the body under cool running water. Cook the crab in boiling water, reducing the heat and simmering for 10 to 15 minutes.

To cook the crab first, plunge the crab into boiling water. Wait for the water to return to a boil, lower the heat, and simmer for 15 to 20 minutes.

OTHER CRABS

Of all the other crabs, perhaps the southern stone crab is best known. Euell Gibbons had a fondness for them: "There is no finer seafood in existence," he wrote. Usually just the claws of these crabs are found in fish markets; unlike the blue and Dungeness crabs, these have huge claws that resemble those of a lobster.

The Alaskan king crab also has huge claws, which make it to most marketplaces frozen. Still sweet, the claws lack the firmness of fresh meat, which suffers from refrigeration. Thaw and use in recipes in which taste is more important than texture. You can also broil the large legs as if they were lobster, just with melted butter and a squeeze or two of fresh lemon.

Virtually every coast in the United States has at least one species of edible crab offshore. Not all of them appear in the markets, though (see "Crabbing," page 20). New England has two crabs, the rock crab and the Jonah crab; Hawaii has a few, most notably the Samoan crab and the Kona crab. The West Coast boasts the red crab, also known as the sea crab, and the South maintains its reputation for green crab, although its known most for its scrapping ability not its flavor.

All of these crabs can be cooked and the meat used for the recipes that follow. Many of these other species produce good soft-shell crabs, too.

Frozen king crab is a suitable alternative for heated casseroles and one-pot dishes.

Judd Pilossof

CRAB, SHRIMP, AND OKRA GUMBO

Creole cooking is a blend of Indian, Spanish, French, English, African, and American cooking. The best-known Creole dish in the United States, gumbo, a cross between a thick soup and a thin stew, is characteristic. The origin of the name is not clear. Some believe it is the African word for okra—ngombo. The Choctaw Indian word for sassafras, from which filé powder is made, is kombo. If you choose to use filé, which is available in specialty stores (see Appendix Two), you'll be that much closer to the real thing.

1 pound blue crab meat
1 pound raw shrimp, shelled and deveined
1 dozen oysters
3 tablespoons butter
1 large onion, chopped
1 green pepper, seeded and chopped
Crush dried red pepper to taste
1 garlic clove, minced
1 quart chicken stock or broth
15-ounce can stewed tomatoes
6-ounce can tomato paste
1 tablespoon chopped fresh parsley
$1/2$ teaspoon dried thyme
$1/2$ teaspoon dried rosemary
$1/4$ teaspoon cayenne pepper
1 bay leaf
12 okra, sliced
1 lemon, sliced
3 cups cooked rice

Remove any remaining shell or cartilage from the crab meat. Cut the large shrimp in half. Shuck oysters and put aside on a layer of aluminum foil on ice, covered, in the refrigerator. In a heavy 4- to 5 -quart Dutch oven, melt the butter. Add the onion, green pepper, garlic, and hot pepper. Cook, stirring constantly, until tender and lightly browned. Add the chicken stock gradually. Add the tomatoes, tomato paste, parsley, thyme, rosemary, cayenne, and bay leaf and bring to a boil. Simmer for 30 minutes. Add the okra and shrimp; cover and cook for 20 minutes. Add the crab meat, oysters and lemon slices and cook for 25 minutes more. Remove the lemon slices. Serve ladled over mounds of cooked rice in deep soup bowls. **Serves 6.**

Variation: Replace the oysters with half a pound of crab meat.
Note: If you use filé powder, substitute 1 tablespoon of the powder for the parsley, thyme, rosemary, cayenne, and bay leaf.

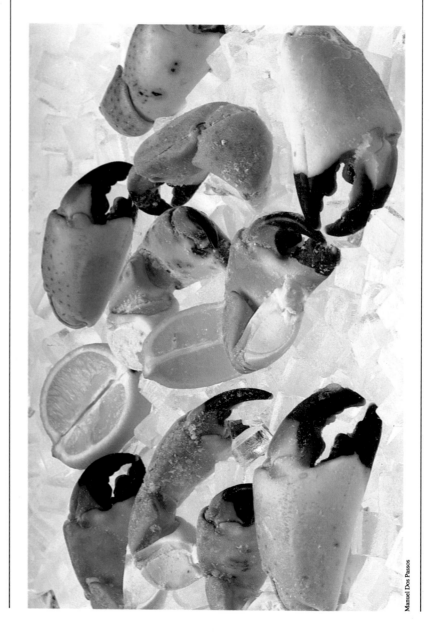

Manuel Dos Passos

Crabs and larger crab claws are delicious chilled or at room temperature, which makes them good picnic fare. Crack the claws before packing or bring along a lobster cracker.

Blue crabs are so prolific that novices, coached by local rod and reel shops, can often catch a night's dinner in a few hours. For a real treat, steam them in beer and eat immediately.

STEAMED BLUE CRABS THE "TRULY MARYLAND WAY"

The blue crab, known for its "cussedness" as well as its intelligence and strength, lies at the heart of many Maryland meals. The recipe below, adapted from The Maryland Outdoor Recreation Guide *and distributed by the State of Maryland tourism office, is simple and scrumptious, the perfect centerpiece to an outdoor dinner.*

½ cup seafood seasoning
½ cup salt
3 cups white vinegar
3 cups beer or water
3 dozen live (and lively) Maryland blue hardshell crabs

Mix the seasonings, vinegar, and beer well. Put half of the crabs in a very large pot with a rack and a tight-fitting lid.* Pour half the seasoning mixture over the top. Add the rest of the crabs and remaining liquid. Steam, covered, until the crabs turn bright red, about 20 or 30 minutes. Serve hot or cold. Serve immediately if they are to be eaten hot; bring to room temperature and refrigerate until ready to serve, for a cold meal. **Serves 9 to 12, depending on the size of the crabs.**

Note: Do not store live crabs with cooked crabs.

*If two pots are used, layer the crabs and divide the seasoning mixture accordingly.

National Museum of American Art, Smithsonian Institution

Lobster

Lobster meat has a reputation unsurpassed on the East Coast. Fresh from the sea, lobsters are indeed food for the gods. Steam them simply and serve with lemon butter. For a more complex dish, you can broil and stuff them; make them into soufflés, stews, and salads; and even use their meat to make a parfait.

To steam them, place the lobsters in 1 to 2 inches of boiling sea water or salted water in a lidded pot. Lower them into the water head first and cover; don't be shocked if the tail flaps once or twice. When the water comes to a boil again, lower the heat to a medium boil and time for 14 to 16 minutes for the first pound, 3 to 4 minutes for each half pound thereafter. Rinse the lobster under cold running water, split, and serve or remove the meat.

Boiling produces similar results, although some sources say the meat is slightly firmer when steamed. As with so many seafood preparations, the choice is yours, and only experience will tell you which is best. Put just enough water in the pot to cover the lobsters; add about 2 or 3 teaspoons of salt per quart of water and bring to a boil. Place the lobsters in the pot one at a time, cover, and cook at a low boil for 7 minutes for the first pound, 2 to 3 minutes thereafter. Rinse and the lobster is ready to be split.

To properly broil a lobster, you should kill the crustacean first, by inserting a sharp, pointed knife into the middle of the shell back at the head down to where the tail joins the body. Put pressure on the knife so the blow is quick and clean; the cut will kill the lobster instantly. You may want to use a glove or a dish towel to protect the hand that's holding the lobster. If the tail flaps, don't be shocked; it's just the muscles working overtime.

Split the lobster following the illustrated instructions, but keep the small legs on. You can either keep the claws intact or crack them off and lay them alongside the body. Crack the claws—either on or off—with a mallet or other hard object to expose the meat. Prepare a small amount of melted butter for basting and brush on. Broil with the shell about 4 inches from the heat source for 7 minutes; turn and broil the exposed side for an additional 8 minutes, basting once or twice. If the lobster is larger than 1 or 1 1/2 pounds, add a minute or so on each side.

You can also broil a lobster after it has been steamed or boiled. If you do this, cut the initial cooking down a minute or two; then broil the split lobster for about 5 minutes. Baste as above. If the meat looks as if it is overcooking, remove at once.

The South Ledges, Appledore (34 1/4" × 36 1/8") by Childe Hassam.

Broiled lobster should be watched carefully so it does not overcook. Be sure to baste the meat to keep it succulent.

Susan M. Duane

Will the Real Lobster Please Stand Up?

Everyone seems to agree that a Maine lobster is the real thing. Even scientists, who have named the crustacean *Homarus americanus*. The only other true lobster in scholarly circles is the European *Homarus gammarus* (sometimes referred to as *H. vulgaris*, writes Waverley Root in *Food*).

Norway lobsters, which are from western Europe and are smaller than their Maine counterparts, and rock lobsters (also known as spiny lobsters) from the Gulf and Pacific coasts of the United States are also edible and quite good, but their meat is not as tender nor as sweet as the *Homarus* lobsters. Neither of these is a true lobster.

When you add the European *langoustes* and *langoustines* to the list of lobsterlike creatures often referred to as lobsters, it is easy to see why confusion more often than not takes rein. Whether you're eating crawfish or lobster, however, the meal is sure to be outstanding. You'll find proponents for each type of animal, the most famous of which is James Beard, who wrote that "in many ways I find a good *langouste* a far more rewarding dish than lobster, especially cold."

A cold, boiled lobster served with a side of lemon butter or homemade lemon mayonnaise is an elegant patio meal. Serve only the claws and tails (in the shell) for a more simple effect. Casual crowds will appreciate the whole lobster, gleaning the last bits of meat from the body and legs.

To add interest and variety to boiled lobster, crack the shell for your guests and garnish with scallions or coriander.

Gordon E. Smith

John Dominis/Wheeler Pictures

LOBSTER NEWBURG

³/₄ pound cooked lobster meat
¹/₄ cup butter
¹/₂ teaspoon salt
Pinch of cayenne pepper
2 cups heavy cream
2 egg yolks, beaten
¹/₄ cup dry sherry
Toast or rice (optional)

Cut the lobster meat into ¹/₂-inch pieces and set it aside.

Melt the butter and blend in the salt and cayenne pepper. Add the cream gradually and cook, stirring constantly, until the mixture is thick but smooth. Stir a little of the heated sauce into the beaten egg yolks, stirring constantly; then add to the remaining sauce. Add the lobster meat and heat, being careful not to boil the mixture. Remove the mixture from the heat and slowly stir in the sherry. Serve immediately on toast points or cooked rice. **Serves 6.**

LOBSTER CAESAR SALAD

2 lobsters, 2 pounds each
3 garlic cloves
³/₄ cup light olive oil
2 cups cubed Italian or French bread
1 large head romaine lettuce
¹/₃ cup extra-virgin olice oil
1 tin anchovies (10 to 12 fillets)
2 tablespoons freshly-squeezed lemon juice
1 teaspoon kosher salt, or to taste
1 teaspoon freshly ground black pepper
1 egg, beaten
³/₄ cup freshly grated Parmesan cheese (reggiano)

Bring a large pot of salted water to a rapid boil and quickly immerse the live lobsters, head first. Cover, return to a boil, and cook for 7 to 8 minutes. Remove lobsters and place on their backs; split end to end with heavy shears or a large knife. Set aside the tomalley (the green liver) and the coral roe (if there is any).

Halve the garlic cloves, press, and place in a heavy skillet with the light olive oil. Place over a medium flame and add the cubed bread when the oil is hot. Turn the croutons as they become golden brown so that all sides are evenly colored. It is important to be attentive, as they will burn easily. When done, drain on paper towels and set aside.

Wash and trim the romaine and dry thoroughly. Rip into largish pieces and place in a large salad bowl. Tear or slice the lobster tail and claw meat into 1- to ¹/₂-inch pieces and add to the romaine. Pour on the extra-virgin olive oil and toss thoroughly until the romaine and lobster are evenly coated. Add the anchovies, lemon juice, salt, and pepper. Toss well again. Drop in the croutons and drizzle on the well-whisked egg (and 1 tablespoon each of tomalley and roe, if desired) and toss again. Finally, add the Parmesan, toss again, correct seasoning, and serve. **Serves 4.**

Sandra Dos Passos

For a more picturesque presentation, remove the mussels from the shells and scrub the shells thoroughly before replacing the meat.

Mussels, steamed with wine and vegetables, are a quick meal for a buffet. Served as shown, the shellfish requires little preparation time.

Mussels

Mussels for a long time were neglected on the coasts of the United States when in Europe they were eaten whole-heartedly. Some of this behavior may be explained by the red tides that make the morsels poisonous. That's only a guess. The red tides on the East Coast—from Maine to Cape Hatteras—are not always dangerous, but you should *always* check with local fishing authorities for their latest reports. On the West Coast, mussels should not be eaten from May through October, during the season of phosphorescence.

Scrub the mussels with a stiff brush or wire pad; cut off the beard if you'll be using the shell for presentation. Place the mussels in a large container of water for an hour to get rid of any remaining sand. Steam these in dry white wine or water with a bay leaf, parsley sprig, and onion for approximately 6 minutes.

To fry mussels, follow the appropriate directions for clams.

There are also many recipes for mussels baked, served cold, and sautéed.

COLD MUSSELS WITH FRESH HERB SAUCE

1 cup Ruffino Orvieto Classico
1 cup cold water
2 leafy basil sprigs, or 1 teaspoon dried basil
1 slice onion, 1/2-inch-thick
1 piece orange rind, 3- by 1/2-inch-thick
2 pounds large mussels (about 2 dozen), soaked, scrubbed, and beards
    removed
Fresh Herb Sauce
Fresh basil sprigs or scallion for garnish

Bring the wine, water, basil, onion, and orange rind to a boil over high heat in a large saucepan; stir. Add the mussels and turn the heat to low. Cook, covered, until the mussel shells open, about 4 minutes. Pour the mussels and cooking liquid through a strainer set over bowl. Set the mussels and orange rind aside.

Return the cooking liquid to the saucepan being careful to leave behind any grit or sand in bottom of bowl. Bring to a boil over high heat. Cook until reduced to 1 cup, about 15 minutes. Refrigerate until chilled.

Pull the mussel shells apart. Carefully separate the mussels from shells using the tip of a knife. Discard half of each mussel shell. Set the mussel into each remaining shell. Arrange on a platter. Drizzle 1/2 cup of the chilled mussel cooking liquid over the mussels (reserve the remaining liquid to make the Fresh Herb Sauce). Cover tightly with plastic wrap and refrigerate for several hours. **Serves 6 as an appetizer, 2 as an entrée.**

FRESH HERB SAUCE

1/3 cup scallions, coarsely chopped
1/3 cup loosely packed basil leaves
1/4 cup parsley, preferably flat-leafed (Italian)
Orange zest reserved from broth, coarsely chopped
1/2 cup chilled cooking liquid from mussels
1/4 cup olive oil
Salt and freshly ground black pepper to taste
Few drops Tabasco to taste

Combine the scallions, basil, parsley, and orange zest in a food processor or blender. Finely chop, stop motor; scrape down side of bowl with a rubber spatula as necessary. With motor running, add mussel broth one tablespoon at a time, scraping down sides of bowl as necessary. Again with motor running, add one tablespoon of olive oil at a time until combined. Spoon mixture into a small bowl; add salt, pepper, and Tabasco to taste. Refrigerate, covered, until well chilled. Spoon a small amount of sauce on top of each mussel. **Makes about 2/3 cup.**

Variation: If fresh basil is not available, substitute 1/3 cup of flat-leaded parsley and 1 tablespoon of dried basil. Omit the 3 tablespoons of flat-leafed parsley in the original recipe. Proceed as the recipe directs.

MUSSELS WITH RAVIGOTE SAUCE

1 teaspoon prepared mustard
1 teaspoon chopped tarragon
1 teaspoon chopped parsley
1 teaspoon snipped chives
3 teaspoons rice wine vinegar
$1/2$ teaspoon salt
4 grinds fresh pepper
1 hardboiled egg, chopped
4 tablespoons olive oil
$2^1/2$ pounds mussels, cleaned and debearded
$2/3$ cups dry white wine

Combine all of the ingredients except the olive oil, mussels, and wine. Whisk briskly, then add the olive oil a tablespoon at a time. Whisk until well combined. Set aside while preparing the mussels.

In a covered pot, steam the mussels in the white wine for about 6 minutes, until opened. Discard any that are still shut. Remove the mussels from their shells, cleaning half of the shells to be used as serving vessels. Replace one mussel to each half shell and top with room temperature ravigote sauce. Arrange 4 or 5 on a bed of greens. **Serves 8 to 10 as a first course.**

Sandra Dos Passos

Mussels purchased from a reputable store or collected with permission from local seashore officials are safe, relatively inexpensive, and delicious. They must, however, be scrubbed and debearded (the "beard" of the mussel can be clipped with scissors).

Oysters

Take your pick: Oysters can be eaten raw, poached, pan-fried, deep-fat fried, broiled, baked, even pickled. Boiling is the only procedure not recommended for these plump morsels.

Practically every coast of the United States and Europe, plus Japan and Australia boast oysters, but the numbers have been decreasing. These bivalves have come into fashion again, and we are eating up the supply at such a rate that we also have to rely on imported canned versions.

Up until a few years ago, oysters were named for where they were grown; to a certain extent this is still true, but the tradition is changing. So, once bluepoint oysters were farmed only off the shore of Long Island. Now the market is widening and the term *bluepoint* defines a type and size of oyster, one that is raised nearby the eponymous town and that measures about 3 or 4 inches across. All the original United States oysters are of the species *Crassostrea virginica,* except for the tiny Olympia oyster, which is like the flat European oyster, *Ostrea lurida.*

An oyster's taste comes from its original seed *and* from its environment. Which is the best is often debated. Opinions and passions intermingle much as they do when wine connoisseurs argue over the merits of their favorites. Many people consider the Olympias from Washington to be the best, although the Chesapeake (Kent and Chincoteague) and Cape Cod (Wellfleet and Cotuit) oysters draw crowds. Belon oysters from Maine and New Hampshire are good as are the Malpeques from Canada.

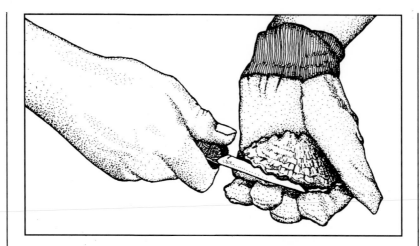

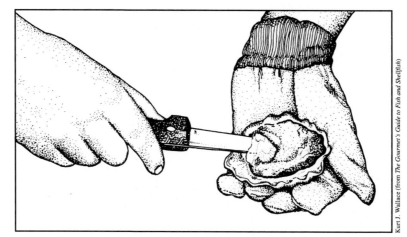

Kurt J. Wallace (from *The Gourmet's Guide to Fish and Shellfish*)

Cultured oysters are gaining popularity. Put together a sampler, just as you might a wine tasting. Choose four or five different types of oysters (two of each per person). Serve with champagne or lemon-scented sparkling water and a loaf of fresh, crusty bread.

Manuel Dos Passos

TO OPEN AN OYSTER

Wearing gloves or holding a towel, approach the oyster shell with caution and patience. Until you get the hang of it, shucking an oyster can be a trying experience. Don't use the edge of the blade to open the oyster, as you would a clam. Rather, use the point and insert into the oyster near the hinge. Twist the knife but be careful not to pierce the oyster. Release the oyster by running the knife around the top of the shell, severing the muscles. Cut the muscle on the bottom half of the shell last.

Save the prettiest oyster shells for individual serving dishes. They are sturdy enough to hold up through a number of washings.

Judd Pilossof

TO COOK OYSTERS

To pan-roast, drain the oysters and place them in a buttered shallow baking dish. Melt 2 tablespoons of butter and add salt and pepper to taste. Pour the sauce over the oysters. Bake at 400 degrees for about 10 minutes, or until the edges of the oysters begin to curl. Serve immediately on buttered toast for a simple treat.

Poaching oysters is even more simple. Put them in a pan with their own liquor and bring to a boil. Remove the pan from the heat and set aside for at least 3 minutes.

Ruth Spear recommends that you poach oysters before frying them. Fry as you would a clam or with flour as your only coating. Broil about 4 inches from the heat source on a buttered baking sheet until brown, about 3 or 4 minutes; squeeze a bit of lemon on them and voila, the dish is done. There are numerous recipes for baked oysters, the plainest of which is to bake in a 475-degree oven with a mixture that is part melted butter, cream, oyster liquor, and flour; flavor with lemon juice, salt, and cayenne pepper.

OYSTERS ROCKEFELLER

Oysters Rockefeller originated in 1899 at Antoine's, the celebrated New Orleans restaurant. Supposedly the richness of the recipe prompted its inventor to name the dish after the richest man he could think of—John D. Rockefeller. Below is just one variation of many.

2 cups fresh spinach
36 oysters in the shell
4 to 5 tablespoons butter
¹/₄ cup chopped celery
¹/₄ cup chopped scallions or shallots
2 tablespoons chopped fresh parsley
2 tablespoons anisette or Pernod
Dash of Tabasco sauce
Rock salt
¹/₄ cup dry bread crumbs
1 tablespoon butter, melted

Wash the spinach, carefully ripping away the stems and discarding the tougher, outer leaves. Set aside. Shuck and drain the oysters, replacing the oyster meats on the deep half of the shells.

In a small saucepan, melt the butter. Add the celery, scallions, and parsley and sauté for 5 minutes. Add the spinach, cover, and cook for another minute or so until the spinach wilts.

Put the vegetable mixture into a blender, food mill, or food processor. Add the anisette and Tabasco and process until almost puréed.

Preheat the oven to 450 degrees. Make a layer of rock salt in pie tins. Place the oyster-filled shells (or ramekins or baking shells) on top. Moisten the rock salt very slightly. The rock salt helps keep the shells in place and the oysters hot. Top each oyster with an equal portion of the spinach mixture. Combine the bread crumbs and the melted butter and sprinkle the mixture equally over the oysters. Bake for 10 minutes. Serve immediately. **Serves 6.**

FRIED OYSTERS

1¹/₂ quarts oysters, shucked and drained
2 cups homemade bread crumbs
1 teaspoon salt
2 teaspoons freshly ground black pepper
4 eggs, beaten
¹/₂ pound butter or lard

Wipe the oysters with paper toweling. Combine the bread crumbs, salt, and pepper. Dip the oysters into the eggs. Lift out and roll in the bread crumb mixture; place on wax paper on a tray or plate. Heat the butter or lard in a deep skillet over a medium to high flame. When the fat is hot, brown the oysters on one side, then on the other. Serve immediately. **Serves 8.**

Fred Lyon/Wheeler Pictures

Though usually baked or pan-roasted, oysters can be just as delicious when cooked in their shells on a grill.

Jeff McNamara

DEVILED OYSTER STEW

5 tablespoons butter
³/₄ cup milk
¹/₂ cup cream
2 tablespoons chopped shallots
³/₄ cup oyster liquid or broth
¹/₄ teaspoon dry mustard
¹/₄ teaspoon nutmeg
Salt and pepper to taste
2 pints oysters
1 cup dried bread crumbs
¹/₂ teaspoon red pepper flakes
2 tablespoons chopped parsley

Melt 3 tablespoons of the butter and add the milk, cream, shallots, and oyster liquid. Mix, then add the mustard, nutmeg, salt, and pepper. Bring the liquid to a boil, reduce heat, add oysters, and let simmer for 2 minutes. Pour into a buttered baking dish. Melt the remaining 2 tablespoons butter and add to the baking dish a 1-inch layer of bread crumbs, red pepper flakes, and parsley; stir until the crumbs are moistened. Spread on top of the stew mixture and bake at 375 degrees for 15 minutes, or until the crumbs are golden. Serve immediately. **Serves 4.**

Scallops

A delightful taste and a firm texture mark the scallop, especially the smaller bay scallops that are found in New England and the northern mid-Atlantic states. As with many other bivalves and shellfish, the farther north you go, the better the quality of the meat.

Steeped in legend and history, scallop lore has continued to fascinate scholars. The account given by Ken Anderson (see "The Shell of Saint James") is only one of many similar but distinct variations. The scallop design has been used in many different styles, from art deco to Victorian and classical themes, in architecture and fine art. In the kitchen, scallops provide serving dishes and lend their name to a method that is now used with potatoes as well as seafood.

Scallop-shaped serving dishes, sold in most gourmet cookware shops, cradle a still-life of shrimp, lemon, and dill. Use the shells, too, for a small portion of poached fish on a bed of greens with a dollop of sauce.

The Shell of Saint James

Coquille Saint-Jacques, the French name for scallop, can be translated literally as "shell of Saint James." (The word *coquille* is applied to nutshells and shell-shaped dishes and kitchen utensils as well as to mollusks.)

The association between the scallop and Saint James, one of the fishermen apostles, dates back to the early days of Christianity. After Saint James was beheaded on orders from King Herod, his remains were believed to have been taken to a site in northwestern Spain—what is now the shrine of Santiago de Compostela. A cathedral was erected over the grave site in the early ninth century; it attracted pilgrims from throughout western Europe.

As Saint James was the patron saint of both the shellfish and the gatherers of shellfish, pilgrims journeying to Santiago de Compostela wore scallop shells as badges. Scallop-shell badges later were worn by crusaders on their way to the Holy Land. During the Middle Ages it was a crime to harm a pilgrim wearing a scallop-shell badge. Santiago de Compostela became known as the Mecca of Spain, and King Ferdinand and Queen Isabela, better known for their aid to Christopher Columbus' New World ventures, erected a hospice for pilgrims near the cathedral.

Coquille Saint-Jacques today is used as the name for many scallop recipes. Hence, one may find coquille Saint-Jacques au gratin, coquille Saint-Jacques frites à la tartare, or even coquille Saint-Jacques en mayonnaise, in which case you simply substitute the word *scallops* for the French term.

—Ken Anderson
The Gourmet's Guide to Fish and Shellfish

Real scallop shells also appear for sale now and then. Boil them briefly and rinse in cold water to clean.

Michael Melford/Wheeler Pictures

TO COOK SCALLOPS

If you're ever lucky enough to have scallops in Europe you'll see that there's more to the mollusk than meets the eye in American markets—although that is *very* slowly beginning to change; a few nouvelle cuisine restaurants are providing the coral with the muscle or the "eye," the latter of which is what gets shipped to fish stores and most restaurants in the United States. The directions below are for cooking American scallops without the coral. The only distinguishing fact you should know when reading scallop recipes is that the sea scallop is the larger of the two; bay and sea scallops can, however, be used interchangeably in the following recipe.

Use the basics as described in the beginning of this chapter under "Cooking Fish." Scallops, like other shellfish, are a boon for dieters. They can be broiled with lemon juice until browned or poached in broth, wine, or water. Sautéing and oven-frying are good choices, too. These bivalves have a sweet but relatively bland taste that you may want to liven up with herbs and sauces. Purists will stick to lemon butter and freshly ground pepper.

SEVICHE

2 pounds scallops
4 limes, juiced
Salt to taste
3 small, ripe tomatoes, peeled, seeded, and chopped
2 chili peppers, chopped
2 small onions, chopped
$^1/_3$ cup olive oil
2 garlic cloves, minced
1 tablespoon fresh coriander, minced
1 tablespoon fresh parsley, minced

Rinse the scallops and drain. If using large scallops, cut in half or in quarters. Place the scallops in a ceramic or glass bowl and pour the lime juice over them; refrigerate, covered, for 3 to 4 hours. Drain. Then add the salt, tomatoes, peppers, onions, olive oil, garlic and coriander until well combined. Refrigerate, covered, for 1 to 2 hours more. Garnish with parsley. **Serves 10 as a buffet side dish.**

SCALLOPS WITH LEMON MAYONNAISE

1 egg
1 egg yolk
Pinch salt
1 cup oil
Juice of 2 lemons
1 pound scallops
$^1/_4$ cup dry sherry

In a blender, combine the egg, yolk, 1 tablespoon of lemon juice, and salt. Blend for a few seconds. Add the oil in a steady stream while the motor is running, pouring it in slowly. Add the rest of the lemon juice slowly once the mixture has the consistency of thick cream. Refrigerate until ready to use.

   Rinse the scallops and put them in a medium enamel or nonstick skillet. Pour the sherry over the scallops, then add enough water to the pan until the scallops are covered. Poach for no more than 4 minutes. Serve immediately with buttered and parslied linguine for a simple meal. **Serves 2.**

Scallops complement green spinach pasta both visually and gustatorily. Carrots or red bell peppers perk up the presentation even more. If adding scallops to a hot sauce or pasta, undercook by a minute or so; the heat from its accompaniment will finish the cooking process.

Judd Pilossof

Matthew Klein

Shrimp

"In North America, shrimp are the most popular of all crustaceans: shrimp are eaten raw, boiled, barbecued, fried, or steamed, and prepared by many other methods," writes Ken Anderson. Cooking shrimp is an easy task in most cases. For a pound of raw shrimp, bring a quart of water and a tablespoon or so of salt to a boil. Add the shrimp and simmer for 3 to 5 minutes or until they turn pink. (Use the longer cooking time for larger shrimp.) Drain and rinse with cold water. If you will be serving the shrimp with a mild sauce, in an aspic, or as a cold cocktail, use a court-bouillon. You can also boil shrimp, but the meat toughens the longer it is cooked.

Frying shrimp varies slightly from frying bivalves. *The Joy of Cooking* recommends soaking the crustaceans in milk flavored with paprika and salt for 30 minutes, then sprinkling with lemon juice, and rolling in cornmeal. Let dry for about 15 minutes before frying in oil heated to 375 degrees.

Shrimp lend themselves to artful presentation—from a simple half circle around a sauce to elaborate "trees" ready to be consumed with tangy cocktail sauce.

Scampi Sobriquets

Scampi is a name assigned to a crustacean, which is also called Norway lobster or Dublin Bay prawn, although it is technically neither a lobster nor a prawn. It is a nocturnal creature with some of the physical traits of both lobsters and shrimp and lives in the muddy bottom waters of the Atlantic coast from Scandinavia to North Africa. They are sold whole or headless and prepared in the same way as shrimp or crayfish. On French restaurant menus, Norway lobsters usually are identified as *langoustine*.

The name Dublin Bay also is a bit of a misnomer because it was acquired at a time when itinerant seafood peddlers of the Dublin area went to the oceanfront docks to collect the items from fishing boats that were not sold to the established fishmongers.

Although scampi and langoustine dishes are commonly offered in North American restaurants, the crustacean is rarely found in retail seafood shops.

—Ken Anderson
The Gourmet's Guide to Fish and Shellfish

SHRIMP WITH CURRY MAYONNAISE

2 bay leaves
1 teaspoon dried thyme
1 teaspoon black peppercorns
3 pounds medium shrimp
1½ tablespoons hot curry powder
2 cups mayonnaise

Bring 2 gallons of lightly salted water to a rolling boil with bay leaves, thyme, and peppercorns. Add the unshelled shrimp and allow the water to return to a rolling boil. Remove from heat and let the shrimp remain in the water for 5 minutes; remove and rinse with cold water. Chill before shelling and arranging on a platter.

Add the curry powder to the prepared mayonnaise and stir carefully. Let sit, refrigerated, before adjusting seasoning and serving with the shrimp. **Serves 6.**

MAYONNAISE

Mayonnaise will usually thicken slightly in the hour or so after it is finished.

3 eggs yolks
1 teaspoon salt
½ teaspoon ground white pepper
½ teaspoon dry mustard
2 tablespoons fresh lemon juice, or 1 tablespoon vinegar
1¾ cups olive oil

Whisk the egg yolks vigorously with the salt, pepper, mustard, and lemon juice until well blended. (A rotary beater, food processor, or blender are easier but less exact options.) Add the oil drop by drop, whisking hard until the mayonnaise begins to emulsify and thicken. As it begins to do so, the remaining oil can be added more rapidly, but take care that it emulsifies before each addition.

If the mayonnaise is too thick when completed, thin gradually with lemon juice. If it breaks, start with new egg yolks in another bowl, add a bit of oil drop by drop, and then add the curdled mayonnaise very gradually. **Makes about 2 cups.**

Be sure that all shrimp are fully shelled and deveined before adding to a complex dish. As a finger food, shrimp can remain in the shell.

Judd Pilossof

Gordon E. Smith

Jambalaya is a Creole classic that is often served in buffets. If planning to keep it warm over a low flame, make sure the decapods are not overcooked.

A good lime vinaigrette makes a simple sauce for shrimp that wakes up the taste buds. Toss with fresh, barely parboiled green beans or snow peas and bell peppers. Add mushrooms and canned beans for an unusual three-bean salad.

SHRIMP, ORANGE, AND APPLE SALAD

3 large scallions
10 watercress sprigs
2 large green apples
3 Seville oranges
1½ pounds medium shrimp
⅓ cup Cognac
¼ cup sherry
½ teaspoon Tabasco sauce
Kosher salt to taste
Freshly ground black pepper to taste
2½ cups mayonnaise
Red leaf lettuce
1 red bell pepper, julienned

Chop the scallions and break the watercress into 2-inch sprigs. Peel, core, and julienne the apples. Finely grate the zest of 1 of the oranges, squeeze its juice, and set the juice aside. Peel the remaining two oranges and slice thin. Mix together the scallions, watercress, apples, orange slices, and zest; refrigerate.

Bring a large pot of water to a boil, add the shrimp, and remove after the water has returned to a boil for 1 minute. Rinse in cold water, shell, and devein if necessary. Mix together the Cognac, sherry, orange juice, Tabasco, salt, and pepper and pour over the shrimp. Let marinate for 2 hours, then mix with the fruit, watercress, and scallions; fold in the mayonnaise.

Line a bowl with red leaf lettuce, spoon in the shrimp, and decorate with the julienned red pepper. Serve immediately. **Serves 6 as a side dish.**

Judd Pilossof

CHARTS, TABLES, AND CONVERSIONS

LEAN AND FAT SALTWATER FINFISH

FISH	FAT	MODERATE	LEAN
Bluefish		Moderate	
Cod			Lean
Croaker			Lean
Drum			Lean
Eel	Fat		
Flounder			Lean
Grouper			Lean
Haddock			Lean
Halibut			Lean
Atlantic Herring	Fat		
Pacific Herring		Moderate	
Lingcod			Lean
Mackerel	Fat		
Monkfish			Lean
Mullet	Fat		
Ocean Perch			Lean
Pollock			Lean
Pompano	Fat		
Porgy		Moderate	
Rockfish			Lean
Sablefish	Fat		
Salmon	Fat		
Sea Bass			Lean
Sea Trout			Lean
Shad	Fat		
Shark			Lean
Sheepshead		Moderate	
Smelt		Moderate	
Snapper			Lean
Sole			Lean
Striped Bass		Moderate	
Swordfish		Moderate	
Tuna	Fat		
Whiting		Moderate	

RECOMMENDED COOKING METHODS

	POACH	BROIL	BAKE	GRILL	FRY
Bluefish		x	x		
Cod	x	x	x	x	x
Croaker	x	x	x	x	p
Drum	x	x	x	x	p
Eel	x	x	x	x	
Flounder	x	x	x	x	x
Grouper	x	x	x	x	
Haddock	x	x	x	x	x
Halibut	x	x	x	x	x
Atlantic Herring		x	x		
Pacific Herring		x	x		x
Lingcod	x	x	x	x	x
Mackerel		x	x	x	x
Monkfish	x	x	x		
Mullet		x	x	x	x
Ocean Perch	x	x	x		x
Pollock	x				
Pompano		x	x	x	p
Porgy				x	p
Rockfish	x	x	x		
Sablefish		x	x	x	
Salmon	x	x	x	x	
Sea Bass	x		x		
Shad		x	x	x	
Shark	x	x	x	x	
Sheepshead	x	x	x		
Smelt		x		x	p
Snapper		x	x		
Sole	x	x	x	x	x
Striped Bass	x	x	x	x	
Swordfish		x		x	
Tuna	x	x	x	x	x
Whiting	x				x

p=pan-fry, if small fish.
Source: Adapted from The Gourmet's Guide to Fish and Shellfish.

NUTRITIVE VALUES OF FISH AND SHELLFISH

FINFISH	PERCENT PROTEIN	PERCENT FAT	CALORIES per 100 GMS	SODIUM MG
Cod	17.6	5.2	157	60
Croaker	18.5	2.5	98	72
Flounder	18.1	1.4	88	121
Greenland Turbot	16.9	3.5	99	*
Grouper	20.1	1.0	89	83
Haddock	18.2	0.5	77	98
Halibut	18.7	4.3	119	156
Mackerel	19.5	9.9	106	33
Mullet	20.1	4.6	122	70
Ocean Perch	14.9	0.7	91	*
Pollock	19.7	1.3	91	*
Salmon	19.9	9.3	163	76
Sea Bass	19.1	1.6	90	67
Sea Herring	17.7	2.8	128	105
Sea Trout	17.7	3.8	123	38
Smelt	17.0	1.4	86	80
Snapper	19.4	1.1	88	90
Sole	16.9	1.4	83	93
Tuna	24.7	5.1	168	63
Whitefish	18.6	5.2	121	53
Whiting	18.9	1.3	90	50

SHELLFISH	PERCENT PROTEIN	PERCENT FAT	CALORIES per 100 GMS	SODIUM MG
Clams	11.0	1.7	63	253
Crab	15.7	2.7	81	330
Lobster	18.1	1.4	98	296
Mussels	11.9	1.4	77	214
Oysters	8.5	1.8	68	386
Scallop	14.6	0.7	78	163
Shrimp	18.6	1.6	209	133
Squid	17.1	1.0	84	158

Data is unavailable.
Source: National Marine Fisheries Service, N.O.A.A.

LIQUID MEASURE EQUIVALENTS

3 teaspoons = 1 tablespoon
2 tablespoons = 1 fluid ounce
4 tablespoons = 1/4 cup = 2 fluid ounces
5 tablespoons + 1 teaspoon = 1/3 cup = 2 2/3 ounces
8 tablespoons = 1/2 cup = 4 fluid ounces
10 tablespoons = 2/3 cup
12 tablespoons = 3/4 cup
16 tablespoons = 1 cup = 8 fluid ounces
2 cups = 16 fluid ounces = 1 pint
4 cups = 32 fluid ounces = 1 quart
8 cups = 64 fluid ounces = 1/2 gallon
4 quarts = 128 fluid ounces = 1 gallon

METRIC CONVERSION TABLE

TO CHANGE	TO	MULTIPLY BY
teaspoons	milliliters	5
tablespoons	milliliters	15
fluid ounces	milliliters	30
ounces	grams	28
cups	liters	0.24
pints	liters	0.47
quarts	liters	0.95
gallons	liters	3.8
pounds	kilograms	0.45
Fahrenheit	Celsius	5/9 after subtracting 32

SOURCES

FOOD

Bettistella's
910 Touro Street
New Orleans, Louisiana 70116
Gulf waters seafood

Blue Channel Company
Box 128
Port Royal, South Carolina 29935
Blue crabs, she-crab soup, crab meat

California Sunshine Fine Foods, Inc.
144 King Street
San Francisco, California 94107
Caviar

Caviar Direct
524 West 46th Street
New York, New York 10036
1-800-472-4456

Clambake International
8 Greenview Street
Suite 15
Framingham, Massachusetts 01701
Live lobsters, steamer clams

Downeast Seafood Express
Box 138
Brooksville, Maine 04617
Live lobster

Ekone Oyster Company
Star Route
Box 465
South Bend, Washington 98586
Smoked oysters

Epicured Smoked Fish
10576 Metropolitan Avenue
Kensington, Maryland 20895
Smoked sea scallops and smoked fish

Flying Foods
43-43 Ninth Street
Long Island City, New York 11101
Seafood of all kinds

Halvorson's Fish Products
8290 South Tacoma Way
Tacoma, Washington 98499
Canned West Coast seafood

Kenyon's Cornmeal Company
Usquepaugh, Rhode Island 02892
Johnny Cake Cornmeal

Longfellow Seafood
and Catering Company
1506 East Republican
Seattle, Washington 98112
Dungeness crab

Maine Edible Seaweed
Larch and Jan Hanson
P.O. Box 15
Steuben, Maine 04680
Maine seaweed

Maison Glass
52 East 58th Street
New York, New York 10022
Various gourmet products

Merchant Adventurers
Tea & Spice Company
70 Hollins Drive
Santa Cruz, California 95060
Caviar

Murray's Sturgeon Shop
2429 Broadway
New York, New York 10024
Smoked fish

Pasta Productions
12358 SW 117 Court
Miami, Florida 33186
Squid ink pasta

Saltwater Farm
York Harbor, Maine 03911
Live lobsters, clams

Smith Knaupp Company
1-800-327-7723 (outside of Florida)
305-977-6666 (in Florida)
Florida seafood

Triple M Seafood
1-800-722-0073 (nationwide)
1-800-323-0073 (in Florida)
Southern seafood plus some

Vieux Carré Foods, Inc.
P.O. Box 26956
New Orleans, Louisiana 70186
Gumbo fillet

York Harbor Export, Inc.
P.O. Box 737   Varrell Lane
York Harbor, Maine 03911
Belon oysters

UTENSILS AND COOKWARE

Williams-Sonoma
Mail Order Department
P.O. Box 7456
San Francisco, California 94120–7456

Zabar's
2245 Broadway
New York, New York 10024

Miscellaneous

The Perfect Setting
122 Hoodridge Drive
Pittsburgh, Pennsylvania 15228
Handmade aprons, quilted picnic basket liners, umbrella table cover, placemats

Le Jacquard Français
200 Lover's Lane
Culpeper, Virginia 22701
Tableware, terra cotta candle pots, etc.

Un Jardin…en Plus
24 West 57th Street
New York, New York 10019
Table linens, artificial flowers, dishware

FOR FURTHER READING

Cooking Fish and Shellfish. Ruth A. Spear. New York: Ballantine Books, 1980.

Food in History. Reay Tannahill. New York: Stein and Day, 1973.

Food. Waverley Root. New York: Simon & Schuster, 1980.

The Gourmet's Guide to Fish and Shellfish. Ken Anderson. New York: William Morrow and Company, Inc. (Quill), 1984.

James Beard's Fish Cookery. James Beard. Boston: Little, Brown, 1956.

Keeping the Catch. Kenn and Pat Oberrecht. Tulsa, Okla.: Winchester Press, 1981.

Miss Manners' Guide to Excruciatingly Correct Behavior. Judith Martin. New York: Atheneum, 1982.

Pierre Franey's Kitchen. Pierre Franey. New York: Ballantine Books (A Fawcett Columbine Book), 1982.

Stalking the Blue-Eyed Scallop. Euell Gibbons. New York: David McKay Company, Inc., 1964.

INDEX

Page numbers in italics refer to captions, illustrations, sidebars, and titles of recipes.